# AVANT-GARDE CHORAL MUSIC

*An Annotated Selected Bibliography*

by

JAMES D. MAY

The Scarecrow Press, Inc.

Metuchen, N.J. 1977

Library of Congress Cataloging in Publication Data

May, James D 1929-
Avant-garde choral music.

1. Choral music--Bibliography. I. Title.
ML128.V7M43 016.784'1 76-30577
ISBN 0-8108-1015-8



Manufactured in the United States of America

To the Memory

of

my Parents

Louis J. and Irene F. May

## ACKNOWLEDGMENTS

To attempt to acknowledge all who have influenced and aided in the production of this book would be an unending task. However, I would be remiss if I did not mention Dr. J. David Boyle, associate professor at The Pennsylvania State University, who as friend and advisor not only offered valuable suggestions and criticism but also gave encouragement from the earliest days when the book existed only as a budding idea for a research project.

In addition I would like to acknowledge the assistance and generosity of the many editors, educational directors, and general managers of the more than fifty publishing companies who so graciously sent scores of their publications for analysis. Many remain anonymous, others I have had the pleasure of meeting; to all, my sincere thanks and appreciation.

Finally, my deepest appreciation to my brother for his quiet yet ever-present interest and support in all my undertakings down through the years.

## PREFACE

This book is the outgrowth of a doctoral research study designed to develop materials to assist the high school choral director in solving some of the problems associated with the selection, study, and performance of avant-garde choral music. Though the abilities of the high school choral group and the music resources of the high school formed the basis for most of the decisions concerning the materials appearing in this work, directors of church choirs, university and college choral directors, and those working with students at the elementary levels of education should find much to assist them in their efforts to incorporate the avant-garde into their programs.

My intention was to develop an annotated bibliography of avant-garde choral compositions readily available from the music publishers of the United States. In noting that the bibliography is "annotated," the reader has a right to expect a great deal more information concerning the entries than a simple listing of title of composition, name of author, name of publisher, and voice arrangement. And a great deal more is provided. Each entry includes the following information: title of composition; name of composer; name of publisher and catalog number; price per copy when available; voice arrangement, including solo parts when required; range and tessitura of each voice part including solo parts; type of accompaniment, with the specific instrumentation required; description of the avant-garde techniques and idioms used in the composition; the characteristics of any traditionally notated music regarding the melodic, harmonic, and rhythmic elements present; description of any supplementary requirements such as staging, lighting, slide or movie projectors, choreography, monaural or stereophonic sound systems; the type of text with its source or author; the approximate performance time when available; and a general classification regarding the difficulty of the composition.

No effort was made, however, to supply any judgment

or evaluation of the musical or artistic worth of the compositions included in the bibliography, nor were any evaluations of this nature made in the decisions concerning the inclusion or exclusion of a particular composition. These latter judgments were based upon criteria which considered the musical resources available to the high school choral director. An effort was made to include as many works as possible, covering the wide range of styles, vocal arrangements, and levels of difficulty contained in the ever-expanding body of avant-garde choral literature.

James D. May

CONTENTS

## Part I

# INTRODUCTION

There have been among the creative artists of every age those whose artistic thoughts required new means of expression. In the twentieth century, the term "avant-garde" has been applied to these originators in the various art fields: music, painting, sculpture, the theatre. Speaking of the musical avant-garde, Ehle writes: "The basic nature of the avant-garde in music is a deliberate, compelling desire and attempt to systematically expand the resources of musical composition."[1]

Following World War II, the use of new electronic and environmental sound materials, new concepts of musical time and space, and new concepts of how and by whom music is made have caused a major upheaval in musical composition. The term avant-garde is now being applied to the specific body of literature which has developed from these new approaches.

Though the sources are varied, many of the early avant-garde developments appeared in the instrumental works of such men as Charles Ives, Edgar Varèse, John Cage, and Henry Cowell. Other instrumental composers, influenced by the ideas as well as by the compositions of these early experimenters, have made these avant-garde compositional techniques and idioms commonplace in instrumental music. Introduction of similar techniques and idioms into choral music has been slower. However, an examination of the recent publications of many music publishing houses reveals that the avant-garde style is becoming more common and more important in the compositions of composers of both sacred and secular choral music.

## Avant-Garde Choral Music

Until approximately ten years ago, most of the avant-garde choral music available had been written for professional performing groups. Those compositions, such as Penderecki's Passion According to St. Luke and Utranja and Stockhausen's Carre and Momente, to mention only four of the better known, are exceedingly complex and difficult to perform. In the past several years, composers have begun to write choral works with the less professional groups, such as high school, college, and church choirs, in mind. While the complexity and difficulty have been reduced and modified, many of the same avant-garde techniques and sounds which appear in the above-mentioned works are employed. An additional body of avant-garde choral music now exists which contains a variety of compositions at every level of difficulty. It is no exaggeration to state that avant-garde choral music now lies within the capabilities of every choral group regardless of their proficiency.

The compositions making up this ever-expanding and more accessible body of avant-garde choral music conform to the basic nature of the style; i.e., they seek to expand the resources of music written for the human voice and the choral ensemble. Avant-garde composers are writing compositions which call for vocal and nonvocal sounds which extend far beyond those sounds traditionally associated with choral music. Tongue clicks and lip flapping, pops and squeaks, moans and groans, laughing and crying, prolongations of vowels and repetitions of consonants are a few of the sounds of the human voice which are being joined to such instrumental sounds as tone-clusters, glissandos, and cluster melodies to create new effects and to develop new forms of expression. Singers are now required to improvise melodies and rhythms, to employ facial and body expression, and to perform choreography as part of their choral experience. Additional sound effects are produced by the singer using his hands and feet as well as other sound-producing materials such as paper, bottles, and metal objects.

Different avenues are being explored by the avant-garde composers. There are works which are entirely avant-garde in nature and other compositions which contain sections traditional in sound and notation juxtaposed with avant-garde passages. Some compositions are to be accompanied by sounds prerecorded on electronic tape while the vocal parts may be either traditional or avant-garde in nature. An exciting body of literature awaits the adventuresome choral director and choir.

Many choral directors, however, are unaware of this body of music and of the wide range of expression, styles, and levels of difficulty contained in it. The number of choirs performing avant-garde music is relatively small. There are a number of reasons why this condition exists. Some choral directors simply have no interest in traveling any but the beaten paths of choral music they experienced during their own musical training. Until such time as these individuals decide not only that it might be interesting and rewarding for them and their choirs to explore new terrain, but that as educators (and every choral director should be an educator of his choir) they have an obligation to do so, little can be done to assist them.

Allowing that many choral directors recognize their responsibilities toward their choir members and to the music of our time, still a number of factors prevent them from studying and performing avant-garde choral music. It is readily recognized that many contemporary compositions make excessive demands upon the capabilities of high school singers, and that this effectively eliminates such works from performance by all except the more exceptional choirs. Zetty does not find this an excusing factor:

> Yet this realization should be no reason to cut off our students entirely from the main flow of creative activity. In order to fulfill his obligations as a teacher of music in the mid-twentieth century, the conscientious choral director must continue to seek out those compositions of artistic worth that are available and that his students are capable of singing. [2]

Many high school directors are actually afraid to attempt contemporary and avant-garde choral music because of their unfamiliarity with the idioms and compositional techniques. Finally, a scanty knowledge of the available published scores of avant-garde choral works contributes to the difficulty.

The present annotated bibliography of published works presents the director with an extensive list of compositions. The annotations accompanying each entry show that there are many compositions at each level of difficulty (easy, medium easy, medium, medium difficult, and difficult) which are not loaded with numerous new techniques or idioms. Some idioms, such as inflected rhythmic speech, make little demand in the way of additional technique on the part of the singer, yet they can serve as a gradual introduction to something new and exciting in choral sound. Director and choir can learn together, going in the direction and at the pace most appropriate for them. All of the compositions in the bibliography are available from dealers and publishers in the United States.

A number of warm-up drills and exercises are suggested to assist the choir in the acquisition of a facility in performing some of the idioms, to help them overcome their inhibitions regarding the new sounds and techniques, and to achieve some of the independence required of the singer by the avant-garde composers. Many choral directors will find that they can devise exercises of their own to aid their singers in acquiring the necessary techniques.

## Criteria for Selection of Compositions

The following criteria were employed in judging whether or not a composition should be included in the bibliography.

Avant-garde. A composition was classified as avant-garde if any of the following compositional techniques were employed:

1. Unconventional notation; i.e., anything other than the traditional staffs, clefs, notes, rests, and dynamic symbols.

2. Choral speaking techniques, such as rhythmic speech, inflected rhythmic speech, or the half-speaking/half-singing voice known as Sprechstimme, whispering, shouting, murmuring, groaning, etc.

3. Unconventional treatment of the text, such as the breaking up of words into their component sounds (the reiteration of consonants, vowels) or the distribution of the syllables of a word among several voices.

4. Aleatory or chance techniques, including improvisation and the ad libitum selection of pitch, dynamics, rhythm, or use of text.

5. Electronic tape accompaniment, either sounding simultaneously with the singers, or at least necessary for the proper performance of the composition. Moog synthesizer accompaniments which are nothing more than an electronic

transcription of traditional types of accompaniment do not satisfy this requirement.

Occasionally a composition was found to use glissandos, finger snaps, hand claps, or similar idiomatic sounds frequently associated with the avant-garde style while the basic style of the composition was completely traditional in melody, rhythm, and harmony. These compositions could often be classified as "pop tunes," "gospel rock," or "rhythm tunes," and as such are not included in the bibliography.

Vocal Requirements. No vocal requirements were adopted for this published version of the bibliography. Each composition is annotated regarding the range and tessitura of each voice part. In addition, the melodic, harmonic, and rhythmic characteristics of the traditionally notated music, as well as a list of all of the avant-garde idioms and techniques employed, are supplied. This should give an indication of the type and degree of vocal proficiency required of the singers. The choral director should be able to judge from the annotations whether or not a composition lies within the capabilities of his group and whether further examination of the score is warranted.

Accompaniment Requirements. The variety of accompaniments used by avant-garde composers is extensive. Consequently one basic criterion was adopted in judging the suitability of a composition for inclusion in the bibliography: Is it reasonable to assume that a high school choral director might have access to the resources necessary for an adequate performance of the composition?

On this basis, compositions requiring a full orchestra of professional stature as the accompaniment were excluded from the bibliography. This eliminated such works as Penderecki's Passion and Utranja, as well as compositions by Stockhausen, Dallapiccola, and others who wrote works with accompaniments requiring this level of performing capability. Compositions written primarily for school or semi-professional orchestras, or which, in the judgment of the composer, can be adequately performed with reduced forces or with keyboard accompaniment, were included.

Compositions requiring smaller ensembles as accompaniment are supplied with annotations detailing the instrumentation required. Here again, the choral director is given enough information to allow him to judge if a composition could be performed with the personnel and resources available.

Some composers have created their own prerecorded electronic tapes to accompany and supplement the choral sounds used in their works. The requirements in this category can range from a single monophonic tape player to multiple sound systems consisting of several stereophonic tape players and speaker systems. These requirements are noted where appropriate.

Supplementary Requirements. There are avant-garde composers who are exploring the multi-media form of artistic expression. They utilize such aspects of a total musical and aesthetic experience as dramatic staging, special placement of the performers, and visual effects obtainable by use of slide-, movie-, and overhead-projectors. Sometimes special lighting is required or at least suggested.

No specific limitations were established in this area of supplementary requirements. Each entry is supplied with information concerning these special features, again allowing the choral director to judge the feasibility of a specific composition, given his particular resources.

## Information in the Bibliography

Each composition appearing in the bibliography is supplied with the following information and annotations when appropriate:

1. Title of the composition
2. Name of the composer
3. Name of the publisher and catalog number
4. Price per copy, when available
5. Voice arrangement, including solo parts when required
6. Range and tessitura of all voice parts including solos
7. Type of accompaniment, with specific instrumentation required
8. Description of the avant-garde techniques or idioms
9. Characteristics of traditionally notated music
10. Description of supplementary equipment, if required
11. Type of text and its author or source
12. Approximate performance time when available

13. Grade of difficulty (easy, medium-easy, medium, medium-difficult, difficult).

## Glossary of Terms

While the meaning attached to various avant-garde idioms is particular to this annotated bibliography, an effort was made to use the terms and to describe the idioms in a manner consistent with what appears to be the evolving terminology or "common practice" among composers and writers of the avant-garde. A number of terms are occasionally grouped under one heading to avoid a proliferation of terms in the annotations. The explanations below indicate when this has been done.

Ad libitum: may be used in reference to pitch, rhythm, dynamics, tempo, or entrance selection; term is used to include "aleatory," "chance," and "improvisation" because of its wider application; (occasionally "improvisation" is used in the annotation since this is specifically called for); in various instances the performer may be supplied with materials such as pitches, rhythms, musical cells or fragments, texts, or he may be required to create his own, i.e., his own rhythm to a supplied melody, his own melody to supplied rhythms, or his own melody and rhythm using a text supplied by the composer.

Aleatory: from "alea," one of a pair of dice; music introducing the element of chance, either in composition or in performance; the performer improvises, creates, acts on his own with the result that each performance is different; term is not used in the annotations.

Approximate pitch: exactness of intonation or pitch not required, only a general pitch level.

Cluster melody: a tone cluster moving in a melodic manner; has a variety of notational forms.

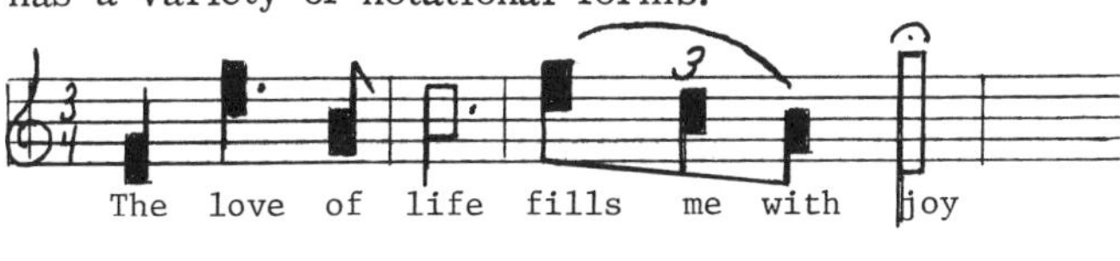


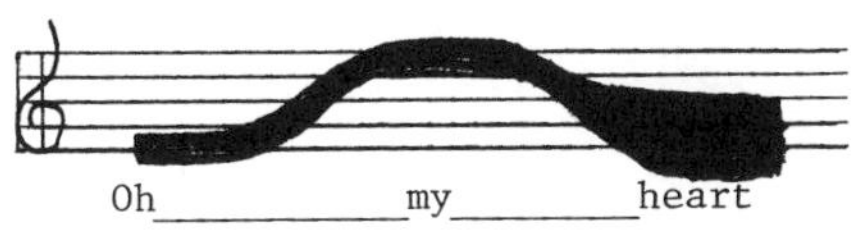

Glissando: sliding audibly, deliberately from pitch to pitch; may be slow or fast depending upon the note values; it may have a specified rhythm or be free; it may be from and to specified pitches or from and to general pitch levels; usually indicated by a slanted straight or wavy line.

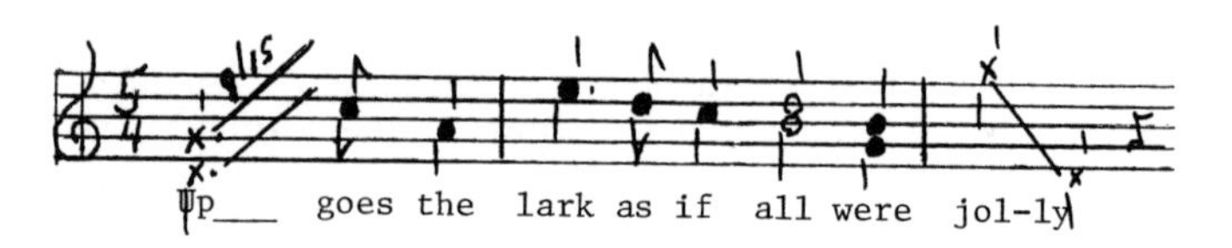


Graphic notation of pitch (melody): general pitch levels are indicated; an approximate pitch is desired, never a specific pitch; might be refered to as "proportional pitch notation"; assume a variety of notational forms; often combined with a graphic notation of rhythm as well.

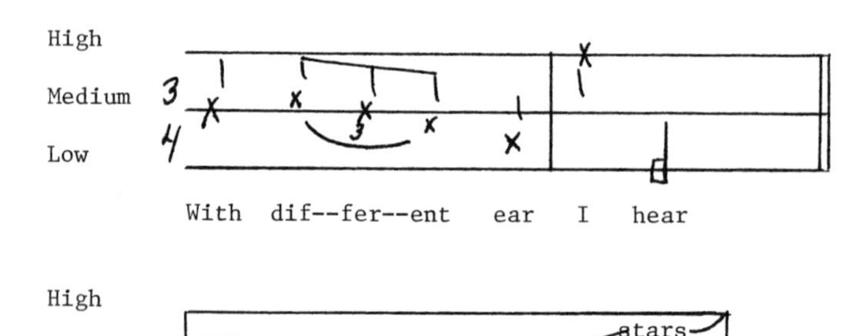


Graphic notation of rhythm (duration): rhythm is indicated by spacing of the notation; time segments which call for an approximation of rhythmic movement; might be referred to as "proportional rhythmic notation"; may use traditional rhythmic symbols or nontraditional ones; often combined with graphic notation of pitch.

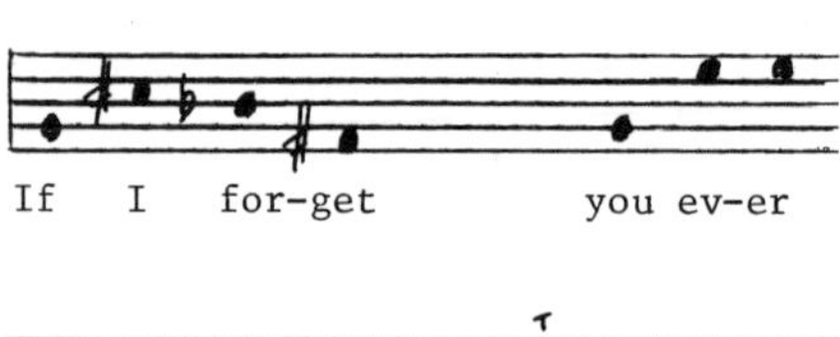


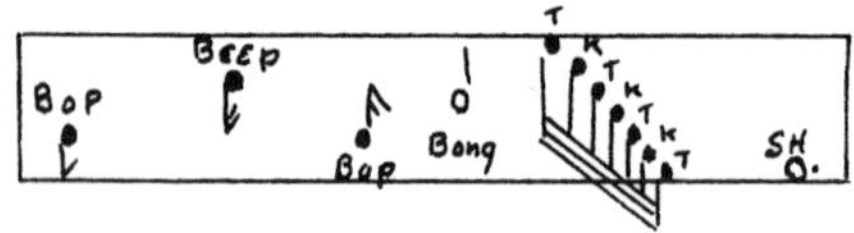

Graphic notation of dynamics: size of the symbol indicates the relative level of intensity of sound; sometimes called "proportional notation of dynamics."

Fragmentation of syllables, words: component parts of a syllable or word are repeated; may be distributed rhythmically in one or several voice parts.

Improvisation: performers are involved in the creative process; may improvise on supplied materials (pitches, rhythms, texts) or use entirely original materials; usually designated in the annotations as "ad libitum."

Inflected rhythmic speech: performers speak the text but use pitch inflections as indicated by the composer as well as the rhythms notated; inflections are always relative with no specific pitch required; appears in combination with traditionally notated melodies to be sung; notational forms vary.

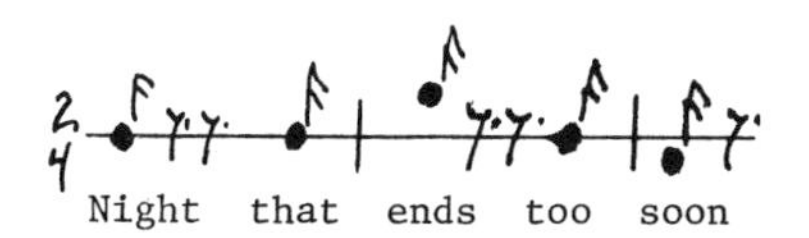


Rhythmic speech: performers speak the text in the rhythm indicated by the composer; frequently combined with traditionally notated melodies.

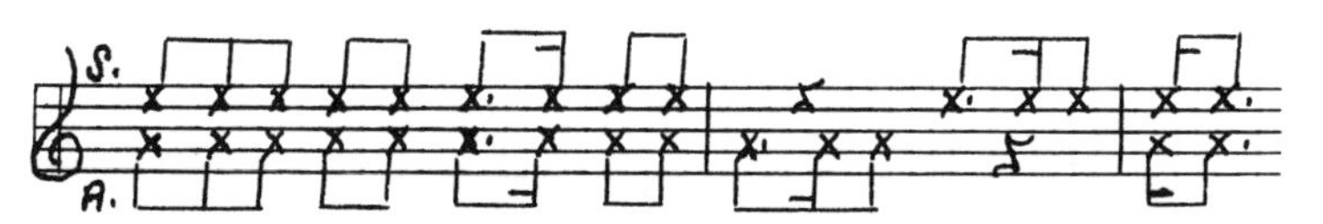

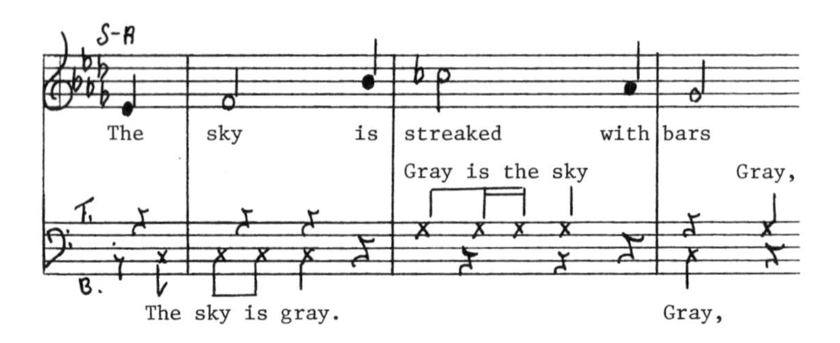


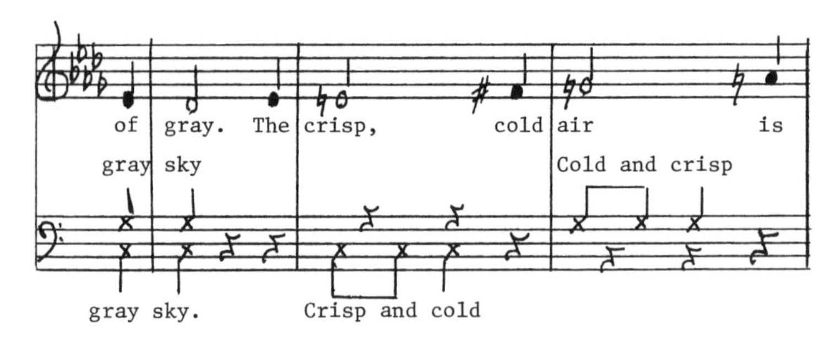


Unvoiced sounds: used by composer to indicate a dynamic and timbre quality combined; whispering, murmuring; consonants sustained; interpretation often depends upon context and text; variety of notational forms.

## Notes

1. Robert C. Ehle, "Romanticism in the Avant-garde: Leon Kirchner's Piano Sonata," The American Music Teacher, XIX (April/May, 1971), 30.

2. Claude Zetty, "Choral Music in the Curriculum: The Choral Music of Paul Hindemith," American Choral Review, XII (January, 1970), 28.

## Part II

# AVANT-GARDE WARM-UPS

The following exercises should assist the choral director and choir in the task of achieving the flexibility, independence, and freedom from inhibitions necessary to perform many of the idioms used by avant-garde composers.

### For Independence

Select a well-known song, such as America, and have each chorister sing the composition through once at his own tempo. Each singer is to hold the final note until all have completed the song. The regular rhythms and pitches should be used; only the tempo is to be chosen by each one independently. It's a fun thing to do, though those who choose a slow tempo usually become a little uncertain towards the end when they find themselves singing by themselves. But this is a first step to independence and a couple of run-throughs should overcome this feeling. At times the effect can be stunning as the song unfolds. Something of this nature can be used to "warm-up" an audience to what is ahead in a concert which includes an avant-garde composition.

Another exercise for independence involves using a short phrase or melody well-known by the choir. Ask each singer to choose his/her own pitch on which to sing the selected passage. Singers need to be encouraged to choose different parts of their range and to avoid unison singing with those around them. Each time the exercise is tried the singers should choose a different starting pitch.

### Glissando

The glissando is one of the more frequently employed idioms used by avant-garde composers. While it is easy to slide from one note to another, it is quite another matter to do so over a specified time span. The choir needs practice singing glissandos at varying rates of speed. This can be done in a number of different ways.

Select an interval: a fifth, an octave, a third, a second. Have the entire choir practice glissing from one of the pitches to the other. They should practice moving in both directions; in time perhaps, the choir can be divided and half gliss up from the lower pitch while the other half moves down from the upper. Use different time values: a quarter note, a half note, a whole note. Of course, the longer the time value, usually the greater the interval span to be covered. Composers usually do not ask a choir to take four beats in a slow tempo to gliss the interval of a second or minor third.

Many choirs have a warm-up of a series of chord progressions. This exercise can be used to practice another way in which glissandos are sometimes used. Have the choir sing through the exercise but gliss from note to note, chord to chord. This will require some sections of the choir to perform a glissando which moves slower or more rapidly than those being performed by other sections, since they will be covering larger or smaller pitch intervals.

Sometimes each singer is called upon to perform a glissando independently of the other singers. To practice this type of glissando, select a tone. Each chorister sings the pitch in a comfortable range. At the conductor's signal, each slides either up or down (the singer's choice), following the conductor's gestures. In time the choir should be led back to the original pitch. A good signal for the conductor is to make a fist with both hands, and hold them together in front of the chest with arms extended somewhat. Then pull the fists apart moving in a vertical direction. The singers choose whether to gliss up or down and the tempo of the glissando. The conductor can move the signal up and down a number of times, varying the distance. Finally he should return to the original position and the choir return to the original pitch. The singers will need to be encouraged to sing with complete confidence that what they are doing is "correct."

## Tone Clusters

The tone cluster is an instrumental sound transferred

to the vocal idiom. It is one of the most commonly used sounds in avant-garde choral music and takes a variety of forms and notations. Besides isolated tone clusters, a composer may write what can be termed a "cluster melody." At other times a "melody" is suggested by a graphic representation which indicates the expansion or contraction of a continuous cluster sound rather than an intervalic shift of the entire cluster as occurs in the cluster melody.

One way to "build" a tone cluster is to have the choir count off by fours, fives, or sixes in each section. All sing a unison in a comfortable range. At the conductor's direction all except the number "ones" move up a half step while the "ones" hold the original pitch. Continue building up by half steps until each number is singing a different pitch. This will serve to get the singers started singing clusters. In time they should be encouraged to sing intervals smaller than a half step and eventually to sing a pitch, however "out-of-tune" it may seem, different from those around them. Practice building clusters within various intervals: a third, a fifth, a seventh. A density of sound is what is desired.

Another approach to the tone cluster is to divide each section into three groups. Have those in group one sing any pitch in their high or medium high range; those in group two are to sing any pitch in their medium range, while those in group three sing any pitch in their low range. This is done in each section. Always the singers are to be urged to select their pitch without reference to the singers around them. There are no section leaders when it comes to singing tone clusters. It will take a few tries before the singers feel comfortable with this after they have spent so many practice hours trying to achieve beautiful unisons, accuracy of pitch and exact intonation. Directors need not fear that singing clusters is going to destroy all that they have worked so hard for in these matters.

The results of Wollman's research, in which he tried to determine experimentally the extent to which a contemporary compositional process based upon aleatory techniques would affect the musicality of nonmusic majors, are of interest in this regard. Some of the aleatory compositional techniques used by Cage, Boulez, Brown, Stockhausen and other avant-garde composers were used by fifty-six nonmusic teacher education students enrolled in a creative activity program. The battery of Seashore Measures of Musical Talents was used as a pretest and posttest. The results showed that there was a significant improvement in the area of tonal memory in the experimental group which used the aleatory techniques, as compared with the control group which did not. From this it might be concluded that singers performing avant-garde compositions might find that their tonal memory is improved and the performance of traditionally notated music enhanced.[1]

## Improvisation

Improvisation is being introduced into more and more choral compositions by composers. Singers are being asked to improvise melodies to rhythms supplied, or to improvise rhythms using supplied pitches. At other times they are given a text and told to express it melodically and rhythmically. There are a number of ways the choristers can be introduced to improvisation.

The pentatonic scale, with its unique quality of sounding "correct" no matter how it is sung, can serve as an introduction to improvisation. The singers should sing the scale up and down, each developing his/her own rhythms. Give them a set number of measures, a meter, and the tempo. Later they can use the pitches of the scale to create melodies as well as rhythms.

A follow-up to this might be to select a well-known melody and have each one select his/her own rhythms. Even more adventuresome would be to use the tune's rhythm but to improvise a new melody to it. Finally, use only the text and have the singers create their own individual musical settings.

Another way of following up the pentatonic scale exercise would be to select a series of pitches (a tone row if you wish) and follow the same procedures with this "scale" or "melody" that were used with the pentatonic scale. As the choir gains experience and confidence, fewer directions or limitations should be given. Eventually the singers should be able to improvise freely, giving full rein to their own creativity.

## Interpretation Suggestions

A primary concept for the choral director studying and

performing avant-garde choral music is that of flexibility. This music must be approached with an open mind, an interest in experiencing the unfamiliar, and a willingness to become involved in "doing" the music. Performing avant-garde choral music becomes a "personal experience" for both the choir and the director. Because few directors have had much previous experience with the style, this also becomes a joint learning experience, something choir and director share.

Acceptance of one basic concept concerning the interpretation of avant-garde notation and the performance of the music will save the director many hours of anxiety and frustration. That is the concept of approximation. Much of the avant-garde notation is graphic in nature and is employed by the composers to indicate only an approximate pitch, rhythm, or dynamic. Just as there is no one, absolute interpretation of any traditionally notated composition, so there is no one, absolute way of interpreting and performing the score of an avant-garde composition. If anything, a greater freedom of interpretation exists.

This is not to say that anything and everything is acceptable. There are certain correct sounds and ways of performing many of the idioms. The comments below offer a basis for some critical evaluations of the choir's execution of some of the more common avant-garde idioms, and suggest ways of obtaining the sounds generally associated with them.

Glissandos should not be delayed until the last part of the beat of the note on which they begin; this results in a quick slide to the next pitch. Rather, the gliss should be extended through the entire length of the time value of the note; it will then resemble what Talley calls "a slow smear of sound."[2]

In singing tone clusters, the singers must be urged to use all parts of their range. Too often the sounds center around a few pitches, so that there are "holes" in the cluster. A density of sound is the desired effect, not merely a dissonant chord. Try to achieve a balanced tone cluster just as you try to achieve a balanced four-, six-, or eight-part chord.

When performing rhythmic speaking parts or sections calling for inflected rhythmic speech, the composer usually intends that the natural quality of the various voice parts be retained; i.e., tenors should sound like tenors, basses like basses, etc. This can be achieved by having the singers use the more characteristic parts of their ranges. Tenors should be speaking on a higher pitch level than basses; altos on a lower one than sopranos.

Although the singers' individual creativity is to be employed at times, the choral director should not hesitate to suggest ways of achieving a more artistic or expressive performance. Suggestions concerning more rhythmic or melodic variation, the use of other parts of the vocal range, modifications in tempo or dynamics should be made as they are needed. At times additional possibilities for expressing the meaning of the text might be offered.

Periodic tape recordings of the rehearsal of avant-garde compositions is strongly urged; it is almost a must. The singers need to hear what they are doing, how the whole "fits together," and what the overall effect is. New insights and ideas will be acquired by the singers which will help them achieve a more satisfying result.

Here are a few caveats Talley offers the conductor new to avant-garde choral music:

> 1. Beware of singing poor vocal technique simply because dissonances are present.
> 2. Beware of singing new notation in a devitalized, uncommitted manner.
> 3. Beware of incorrect syllabic stress because the rhythm appears in a new notation.
> 4. Beware of ignoring composer markings (trust the markings first, then trust the intuition of traditional musicianship).
> 5. Last and most important, beware of a closed mind, or a closed ear; what might be today's 'diabolus musica' may be tomorrow's heavenly muse.[3]

Finally, remember that avant-garde choral music embraces as wide a range of styles and expressions as traditionally notated music. There are works which are profoundly serious in nature, while others are light-hearted. There are some that simply are fun for both the performers and the audience. Just as you would explain the intention and meaning of the composer of a traditional choral work, so you should give the singers some insight to the intention and meaning of the avant-garde composer. The style was chosen for a purpose, and awareness of it will go a long way in achieving the desired effect. All of this, of course, requires a conviction and enthusiasm on the part of the choral director.

## Notes

1. William A. Wollman, "The Effect of a Contemporary Compositional Process Derived from Aleatory Techniques on the Musicality of College Level Non-Music Majors" (unpublished doctoral dissertation, New York University, 1972), p. 65.

2. Mike Talley, "Knut Nystedt's Compositional Style as Analyzed in 'Praise to God'," The Choral Journal, XV (September, 1974), p. 13.

3. Talley, p. 13.

Part III

## ANNOTATED BIBLIOGRAPHY

The annotated bibliography is organized in the following manner. The annotated entries appear in alphabetical order according to title of composition. A list of publishers' names and addresses follows. Included in the list is the code name by which each publisher is identified in the annotated entries. The agent is listed for those companies whose publications are available in this manner.

The bibliography contains a series of indexes of compositions according to voice arrangement. Both a cappella and accompanied works are included in a single list under each voice heading, with the a cappella scores identified by an asterisk. Compositions are listed under the following headings: SATB and combinations of SATB divisi, SAB, SSA (SSAA), TTB (TTBB), two-part (SA, TB, SB), Unison, Speaking Chorus (these works are written for speaking voice and do not involve singing), and compositions employing electronic tape accompaniment either as a necessary feature or as an option.

A composer index is provided which contains the titles of the compositions of each composer included in the bibliography and the page where the annotated entry for each composition is located.

A RIVEDER LE STELLE

Composer: Ingvar Lidholm — Author: Dante Alighieri

Publisher: Hansen — No. WH 130 — Price: $2.50

Voicing: SATB div.;[1] S. solo[2] — Grade: diff. — Time: 14:00

Accompaniment: a cappella[3]

Type of Text: secular; nocturne

Range and Tessitura:

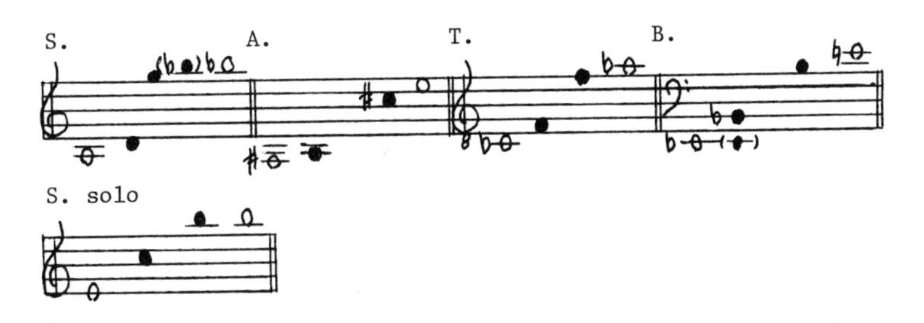


Avant-garde:

glissandos; tone clusters written out

Traditional:

Melody: nontonal; chromatic; disjunct and conjunct; cross voices; melodic fragments repeated

Harmony: nonfunctional; major/minor seconds between adjacent voices (results in cluster effect at times); fourths, fifths; augmented, diminished intervals of various types

Rhythm: changing meters (2/2, 7/4, 9/4, 8/4, 4/4, 2/4, 3/4, 3/2); syncopation; triplet quarters, eighths, halfs; triplet quarters, halfs against four quarters at same time; three-against-two; five eighths to half note beat

---

[1]Choir should number 64; 16 singers to each part; each part divided into four subparts

[2]Soloist sings unmetered obligato; difficult; nontonal; disjunct at times

[3]No reduction of voice parts; as many as twenty staffs

AGLEPTA

Composer: Arne Mellnas Author: Gunilla Marcus

Publisher: Hansen No. WH- 151 Price: $1.00

Voicing: SSA Grade: med-diff.

Accompaniment: a cappella[1] Time:

Type of Text: secular; Swedish proverbs

Range and Tessitura:

Avant-garde:

ad libitum rhythm, tempo, pitch; whispering; glissandos; speaking

Traditional:

Melody: nontonal; chromatics; major/minor thirds

Harmony: nonfunctional; aleatoric; fourths, fifths of various types

Rhythm: unmetered sections; syncopation in 6/8 meter

[1]No reduction of voice parts

ALEATORY PSALM

Composer: Gordon H. Lamb Author: biblical

Publisher: World No. CA 4003-8 Price:

Voicing: SATB; T. solo Grade: med Time: 3:00

Accompaniment: a cappella

Type of Text: sacred; Psalm 150; praising

Range and Tessitura:

Avant-garde:

inflected rhythmic speech; inflected rhythmic speech and singing combined; tone clusters; cluster melody; glissandos; improvisation on supplied rhythms, in response to solo; ad libitum pitch; graphic notation of pitch

Traditional:

Melody: tonal, some chromatics; shifting tonality; augmented, diminished intervals

Harmony: major/minor seconds between adjacent voices; fourths, sevenths

Rhythm: changing meters (5/4, 6/4, 4/4, 2/4); syncopation; triplet quarters, eighths, sixteenths

1Only specified pitch; all others ad libitum

ALIKE AND EVER ALIKE

Composer: Michael Hennagin Author: Carl Sandburg

Publisher: Walton No. 2187 Price: 35¢

Voicing: SATB, four speakers Grade: easy Time: 1:45

Accompaniment: a cappella: electronic tape[1]

Type of Text: secular; serious; humanistic

Range and Tessitura: not applicable

Avant-garde:

speaking with singing; entrances time in seconds;[2] approximate pitches; tone cluster effect

Traditional:

Rhythm: unmetered; traditional rhythmic signs used

[1]Tape available - $10.00; supplies cues for full work: The Family of Man

[2]Stop watch needed

ALL THE WAYS OF A MAN

Composer: Knut Nystedt Author: biblical

Publisher: Augsburg No. 11-9004 Price: 60¢

Voicing: SATB div. Grade: diff. Time: 6:30

Accompaniment: a cappella[1]

Type of Text: sacred; Proverbs: 16, 2-9; 16-20; man's relation to God

Range and Tessitura:

Avant-garde:

rhythmic speech; graphic notation of pitch; tone clusters

Traditional:

Melody: tonal, chromatic; disjunct, augmented, diminished intervals; crossed voices; pitch pipe suggested for cues

Harmony: nonfunctional; major/minor seconds between adjacent voices; unisons

Rhythm: changing meters (4/4, 3/4, 4/3, 3/2, 2/2, 7/8, 5/8, 3/8); triplet quarters, eighths;

two-against-three; chant-like free rhythm section

[1]No reduction of voice parts

ALLELUIA

Composer: Daniel Pinkham  Author:

Publisher: E. C. Schirmer  No. 2954  Price:

Voicing: SATB, 4-8 women soloists[1]  Grade: med-diff.  Time: 6:10

Accompaniment: electronic tape

Type of Text: sacred; one word, "alleluia"

Range and Tessitura:

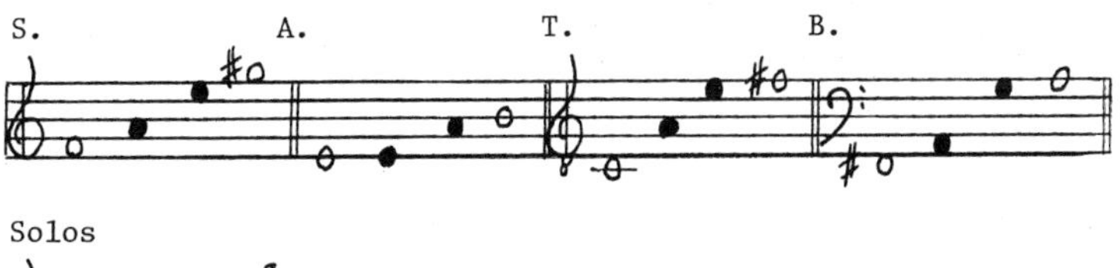

Avant-garde:

ad libitum pitch, tempo, entrances, use of melodic fragments; random speaking; tone clusters; special location of soloists; stop watch essential

Traditional:

Melody: tonal feeling through repetition of melodic passages; shifting "tonality"; conjunct

Harmony: mostly triadic; two triads a second apart sung simultaneously

Rhythm: choral and solo phrases unmetered; choral passages: changing meters (4/4, 3/4, 2/4)

[1]Sets of "antiphonal solos" where singer chooses a phrase to sing, another singer follows choosing complimentary or contrasting phrases, etc.

ALLELUIA - 1973

Composer: Edward Diemente Author: biblical

Publisher: Gray No. GCCS 22 Price: 30¢

Voicing: SAB Grade: med. Time: 6:16

Accompaniment: electronic tape;[1] tape supplies pitch cues

Type of Text: sacred; rejoice in Christ's sacrifice

Range and Tessitura:

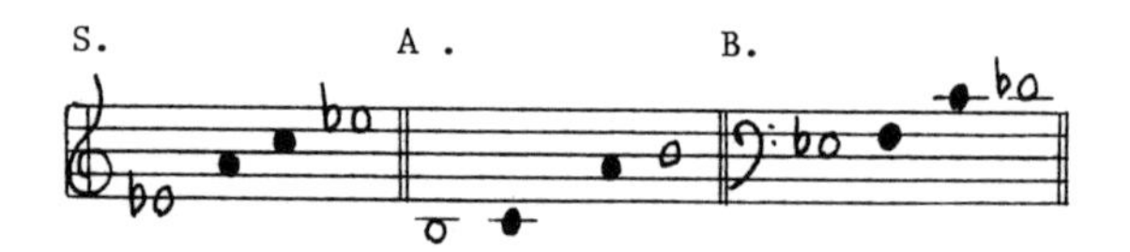


Avant-garde:

singing with electronic tape accompaniment
all music choir performs traditionally notated

Traditional:

Melody: tonal, some chromatics; conjunct

Harmony: nonfunctional; augmented, diminished fourths, octaves; minor seconds between adjacent voices; unisons

Rhythm: changing meters (3/4, 4/4, 5/4, 2/4); much unison rhythmic movement

[1]Tape available - $5. 95; no reduction of voice parts in score

ALLELUIA SUPER-ROUND, AN

Composer: William Albright Author:

Publisher: Elkan-Vogel No. 362-03180 Price: 30¢

Voicing: eight or more singers Grade: med. Time:

Accompaniment: a cappella[1]

Type of Text: one word: Alleluia

Range and Tessitura:

Avant-garde:

each singer performs musical cells independently; modified traditional rhythmic notation

Traditional:

Melody: tonal, conjunct; grace notes

Harmony: aleatoric

[1]Use of instruments optional; play same musical cells

AMERICA, THE LAND OF THE PEOPLE

Composer: Bert Konowitz Author:

Publisher: Alfred No. 6315Z Price: 60¢

Voicing: SATB[1] Grade: med-diff. Time:

Accompaniment: piano[2]

Type of Text: secular; patriotic

Range and Tessitura:

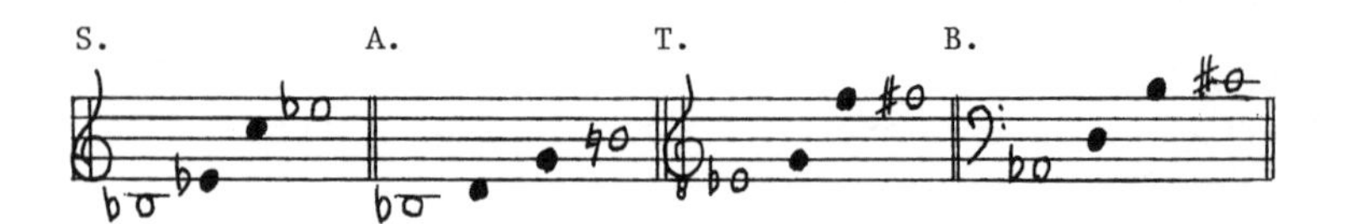


Avant-garde:

rhythmic speech; improvisation (optional; no materials supplied, only text subject suggested)

Traditional:

Melody: tonal; chromatics; chordal patterns; disjunct

Harmony: functional; sevenths of various types; major/minor seconds between adjacent voices; lot of close voicing

Rhythm: changing meters (3/4, 4/4); syncopation

[1]Can be performed as unison, two-, three-, or four-part composition

[2]No reduction of voice parts

AMERICAN DIALOGUE

Composer: Roy E. Johnson  Author: Roy E. Johnson

Publisher: Somerset  No. BR2003  Price: 30¢

Voicing: SATB; solo speakers  Grade: easy  Time: 2:00

Accompaniment: piano; optional guitar (chords indicated)

Type of Text: secular; humanistic; concern for fellow man

Range and Tessitura:

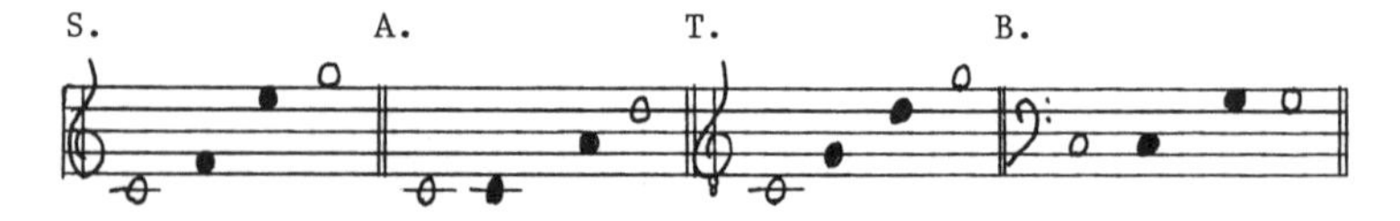

Avant-garde:

shouting

Traditional:

Melody: tonal, some chromatics; ostinatos

Harmony: functional; occasional sevenths; unisons for SAT

Rhythm: syncopation

ANABATHMOS I

Composer: J. D. Weinland Author:

Publisher: Walton No. M-116 Price: $2.00

Voicing: 10 singers[1] Grade: med-easy

Time: 6:30

Accompaniment: violin, viola, cello[2]; 3 sets tubular chimes; metal wind chimes; electronic tape[3]

Type of Text: novelty; vowel sound "oh," "ah"

Range and Tessitura: relative to individual singers

Avant-garde:

graphic notation of pitch, rhythm; ad libitum use of fragments of music, tempo

Traditional: not applicable for chorus

[1]Three soprano, three alto, two tenor, two bases (SATB parts, not divisi)

[2]Strings play long sustained chords

[3]15-second tape delay required; two tape recorders needed; instructions supplied to achieve the delay effect

AND DARKNESS FELL

Composer: Robert Wetzler Author: biblical

Publisher: AMSI No. 266 Price: 40¢

Voicing: SATB div.[1] Grade: med-diff. Time:

Accompaniment: a cappella[2]

Type of Text: sacred; Matt. 27:45-54, events at the death of Christ

Range and Tessitura:

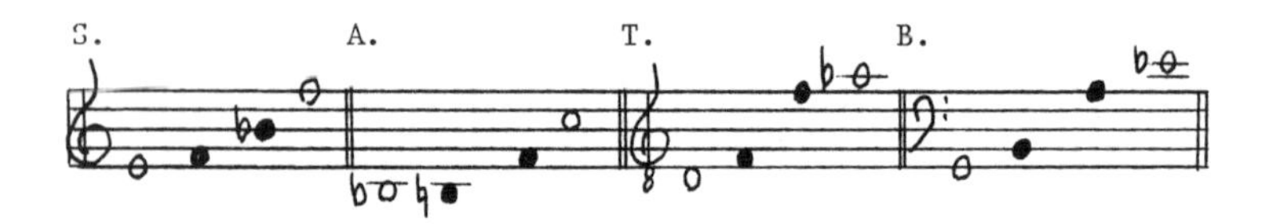


Avant-garde:

rhythmic speech; rhythmic speech and singing combined; written out tone clusters; free trill

Traditional:

Melody: tonal; unisons or doublings in several parts; chromatics disjunct, conjunct when building up tone clusters

Harmony: some sense of function felt with shifting chords against stationary pitch or pitches; major/minor seconds between adjacent voices

Rhythm: changing meters (3/4, 4/4, 2/4); syncopation; combinations of eighths and sixteenths; three-against-two

---

[1]Alto and Bass parts divided into three sub-sections

[2]No reduction of voice parts

ANTIPHONA DE MORTE

Composer: Barne Slögedal Author: Notker

Publisher: Walton No. 2903 Price: 50¢

Voicing: SATB div.; T. solo Grade: med-diff. Time:

Accompaniment: a cappella

Type of Text: sacred; Latin; supplication for mercy after death

Range and Tessitura:

Avant-garde:

rhythmic speech; tone clusters; glissandos; whispering

Traditional:

Melody: tonal; shifting tonalities; chromatics; conjunct

Harmony: functional sevenths, ninths, elevenths in succession; chords with added tones; parallel triads (major, minor, augmented); ostinatos

Rhythm: changing meters (3/4, 5/4, 4/4, 3/2, 2/2); unmetered section; syncopation; triplet quarters; three-against-two

---

[1]Tenor solo eight measures; range: F to A on staff

ASCENSIONS

Composer: Louis F. Davis, Jr. Author: E. H. Adrian

Publisher: Scarborough No. M-127 Price: $1.00

Voicing: SATB, div. Grade: med-diff.

Time:

Accompaniment: electronic tape[1]; piano part supplies duplicate of tape for rehearsal purposes

Type of Text: secular; various stellar constellations

Range and Tessitura:

Avant-garde:

ad libitum pitch, entrances; rhythmic speech; glissandos; whispering; rhythmic speech and singing combined; tone clusters written out

Traditional:

Melody: tonal; long sustained pitches; chromatics; conjunct

Harmony: functional; chords built in fourths; patterns repeated; open fifths in parallel motion; unisons and doublings between men's and women's voices

Rhythm: changing meters (4/4, 6/4, 3/4, 5/4, 6/8); duplet quarters; combinations of eighths and sixteenths; syncopation

[1]Pitch, tempo, and timing cues supplied by tape

ASPIRATIONS

Composer: Harold Owen Author: old speech exercise

Publisher: AMSI No. AMSI 1025 Price: 40¢

Voicing: 6 speakers (choirs) Grade: med. Time:

Accompaniment: a cappella

Type of Text: novelty

Range and Tessitura: not applicable

Avant-garde:

fracturing of words and syllables into component parts; rhythmic speech

Traditional:

Rhythm: traditional notation used; syncopation; combination of eighths and sixteenths

AUTUMN

Composer: John Paynter Author: Gyodai

Publisher: Universal No. UE 15472 Price: 50¢

Voicing: Unison Grade: easy Time: 0:48[1]

Accompaniment: soprano glockenspiel; metallophone; optional violin, chime bars (C, A, G, D); other instruments optional

Type of Text: a Haiku; moods of the season

Range and Tessitura:

Avant-garde:

ad libitum tempo, rhythm; time segments

Traditional:

Melody: sequences of alternating falling minor thirds, rising major seconds

Harmony: occurs by chance because of ad libitum rhythms

[1]Length of composition can be extended

BABEL

Composer: Gregg Smith  Author: biblical

Publisher: G. Schirmer  No. 11793  Price: 60¢

Voicing: SATB; 5 speaking groups  Grade: med-diff.  Time:

Accompaniment: piano (two performers)[1]

Type of Text: sacred; dramatic presentation of story of Tower of Babel

Range and Tessitura:

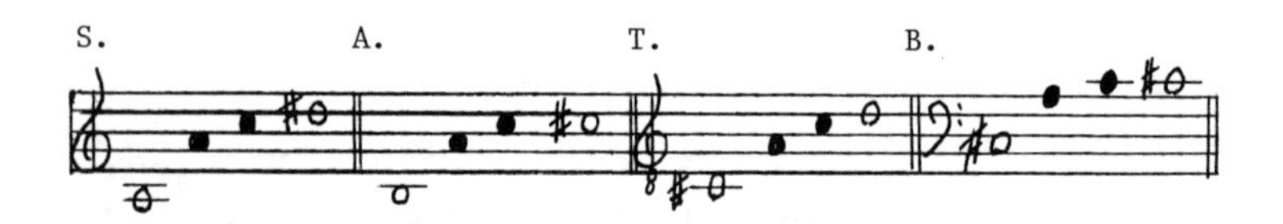


Avant-garde:

inflected rhythmic speech; tone clusters; glissandos; ad libitum speaking; speaking and singing combined; fragmentation of words; graphic notation of pitch, rhythm.

Traditional:

Melody: tonal, chromatics; conjunct; chanting on pitch

Harmony: nonfunctional; repeated progressions give some "functional" feeling; major/minor seconds between adjacent voices; fourths, fifths; much unison singing

Rhythm: changing meters (4/4, 3/4, 2/4); unmetered passages; triplet quarters; much unison rhythmic movement

[1]One pianist needs facility reading accidentals; other must improvise and use the instrument percussively

BE STRONG IN THE LORD

Composer: D. Duane Blakley Author: biblical; Martin Luther

Publisher: Flammer No. A-5637 Price: 35¢

Voicing: (SA(T)B Grade: med-easy Time: 4:15

Accompaniment: organ or piano; optional brass, percussion, electronic tape[1]

Type of Text: sacred; Ephesians 6: 10-17; Romans 8; confidence in God

Range and Tessitura:

Avant-garde:

inflected rhythmic speech; glissandos; ad libitum speaking of text

Traditional:

Melody: tonal; predominantly diatonic scale patterns; modal

Harmony: functional; modal; open fourths; major seconds between adjacent voices

Rhythm: changing meters (4/4, 7/8, 5/8, 2/4); syncopation; combinations of eighths and sixteenths

[1]Brass-percussion parts - $3. 00; tape - $3. 00

BEATUS VIR

Composer: Vagn Holmboe Author: biblical

Publisher: Hansen No. WH-111 Price: 75¢

Voicing: SSATB Grade: diff. Time:

Accompaniment: a cappella[1]

Type of Text: sacred; Latin (English translation supplied); Psalm 1:1-4

Range and Tessitura:

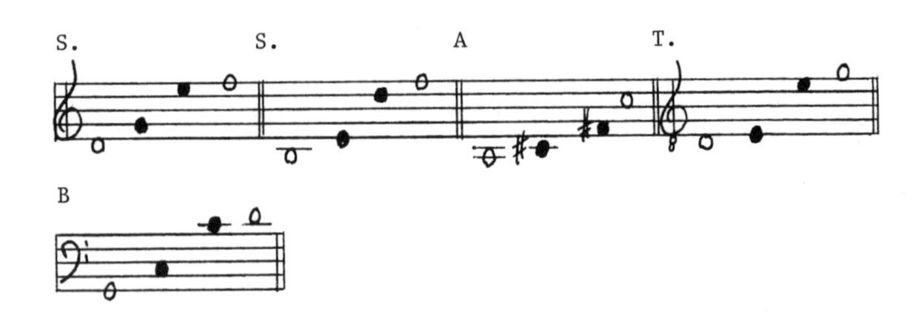


Avant-garde:

glissandos; rhythmic speech

Traditional:

Melody: tonal; shifting tonality; nontonal; chromatic; cross voices; conjunct, disjunct

Harmony: functional; nonfunctional (functional feeling through repetition of patterns); altered chords; sevenths; major/minor seconds between adjacent voices

Rhythm: changing meters (3/4, 4/4, 5/4, 6/4, 8/4); combinations of eighths and sixteenths; syncopation

1No reduction of voice parts

BILOGY, A[1]

Composer: Brock McElheran Author:

Publisher: C. Fischer No. CM 7802 Price: 35¢

Voicing: four-part Grade: easy Time:[2]

Accompaniment: a cappella

Type of Text: secular; novelty; humorous

Range and Tessitura: relative to individual singers

Avant-garde:

cluster melody; ad libitum pitch, entrances; trilled-R; shouting; gestures; sneezing; coughs; yawns; choreography

Traditional:

Brahms' Lullaby and Rock-a-bye Baby used

---

[1]Two compositions: Non-Lullaby; Audiences We've Known and Loved; can be performed separately

[2]Non-Lullaby - 2:15; Audiences - ad libitum time



BLACK CAT

Composer: Christopher Small Author: Christopher Small

Publisher: Universal No. 14659 Price: 35¢

Voicing: unison Grade: easy Time:

Accompaniment: percussion (chime bars, suspended cymbals); xylophone; triangles, maracas

Type of Text: mood evoking

Range and Tessitura: not applicable

Avant-garde:

speaking; sustaining vowels, consonants; graphic notation of pitch, rhythm; ad libitum rhythm

Traditional: not applicable

BLUE WHALE

Composer: Sydney Hodkinson Author: Keith Gunderson

Publisher: Merion No. 342-40101 Price: 40¢

Voicing: SATB/SATB[1] Grade: med-diff. Time: 1.20

Accompaniment: a cappella[2]

Type of Text: secular; novelty

Range and Tessitura:

Avant-garde:

improvisation on supplied pitches; ad libitum whispering

Traditional:

Melody: tonal, chromatics; scale, chordal patterns

Harmony: functional; sevenths, ninths, elevenths; altered chords; chords with added notes

Rhythm: syncopation; suggested rhythms for improvisation include triplet eighths; cross rhythms in slow tempo

[1]One choir improvises throughout; pitches, tonalities supplied; rhythms suggested; other choir sings traditionally notated music and performs random whispers (at conclusion)

[2]No reduction of voice parts

BUFFALO BILL

Composer: James Yannatos Author: e. e. cummings

Publisher: AMP No. A-646 Price: 30¢

Voicing: TTBB Grade: diff Time:

Accompaniment: a cappella

Type of Text: secular; novelty

Range and Tessitura:

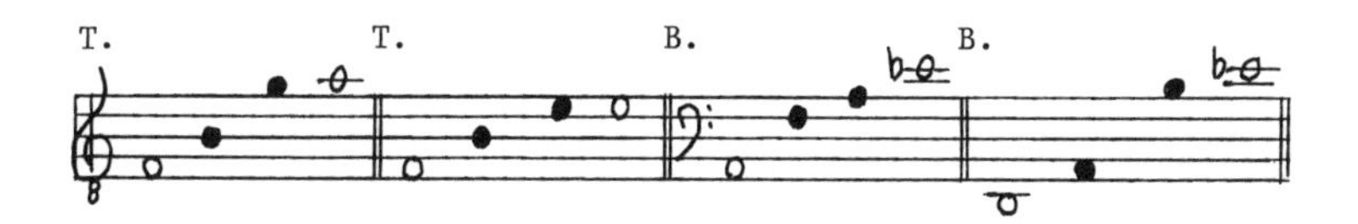


Avant-garde:

rhythmic speech, whispering; inflected rhythmic speech; glissandos; shouting; finger snaps

Traditional:

Melody: tonal; disjunct; small fragments

Harmony: nonfunctional; chords with added tones

Rhythm: triplet eighths, sixteenths; combinations of eighths and sixteenths

BUMBLE BEE, THE

Composer: Sven-Erik Bäck Author: Folke Isaksson[1]

Publisher: Hansen No. WH-127 Price: $1.25

Voicing: SATB Grade: diff. Time:

Accompaniment: cello, piano/celesta (same part for either instrument); suspended cymbal; maracas; gongs; triangle; bells; snare drum; tam-tam, bongos; xylophone; vibraphone; claves; woodblock[2]

Type of Text: secular; novelty; vowels, consonants

Range and Tessitura:

Avant-garde:

tone clusters; inflected rhythmic speech; glissandos; cluster melody; approximate pitch

Traditional:

Melody: nontonal, chromatic; repetitions on same pitch; disjunct

Harmony: nonfunctional; major/minor seconds between adjacent voices; close voicing; unisons and octave doublings; altered chords; sevenths

Rhythm: changing meters (3/4, 5/8, 4/4, 2/4, 6/8); triplet eighths, quarters; syncopation; combinations of eighths and sixteenths

[1]English text by Gunilla Marcus

[2]Keyboard improvises, plucks piano strings; needs more than one percussionist; cellist needs facility; no reduction of voice parts

BURST OF APPLAUSE

Composer: Vito E. Mason Author:

Publisher: Gentry No. B-201 Price: 30¢

Voicing: four-part choir[1] Grade: easy Time: 0:30

Accompaniment: not applicable

Type of Text: not applicable

Range and Tessitura: not applicable

Avant-garde:

exploration of musical elements through applause; graphic notation of pitch, rhythm, dynamics

Traditional: not applicable

[1]Should be fairly large group

CALL OF ISAIAH, THE

Composer: Daniel Pinkham Author: biblical

Publisher: Ione No. 2911 Price: 35¢

Voicing: SATB[1] Grade: Diff. Time: 4:35

Accompaniment: electronic tape;[2] organ;[3] optional timpani, giant tam-tam, suspended cymbal, triangle

Type of Text: sacred; Isaiah 6:1-9; holiness of God

Range and Tessitura:

Avant-garde:

inflected rhythmic speech; graphic pitch notation; ad libitum pitch, timbre, selection of music cells; tone clusters; glissandos

Traditional:

Melody: nontonal, chromatic; occasional sevenths, diminished fourths

Harmony: nonfunctional; dissonant; major/minor seconds between adjacent voices moving in parallel motion

Rhythm: changing meters (4/4, 9/8, 8/8, 2/4); unmetered sections; triplet eighths, sixteenths; syncopation

---

[1]Can be performed with 4-part men or 4-part women group

[2]Available from publisher

[3]Does not duplicate voice parts

CANINE COMMANDMENTS

Composer: G. Alan Smith Author: G. Alan Smith

Publisher: Gentry No. G-256 Price: 40¢

Voicing: SSATB Grade: diff. Time: 1:15

Accompaniment: a cappella[1]

Type of Text: secular; novelty

Range and Tessitura:

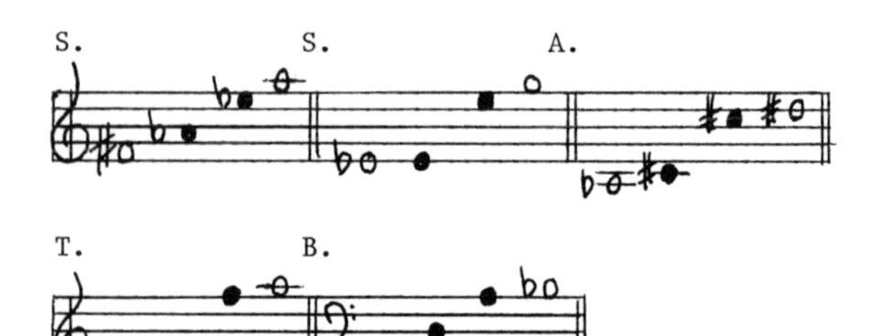


Avant-garde:

fragments of syllables; glissandos; graphic notation of pitch; ad libitum tempo

Traditional:

Melody: nontonal, chromatics;[2] disjunct; cross voices

Harmony: nonfunctional; seconds between adjacent voices

Rhythm: syncopation; sixteenths; grace notes indicate performance of consonants

[1]No reduction of voice parts

[2]Composer states: "Exact pitches are important though not crucial to the success of the performance."

CANON AND CODA[1]

Composer: Brock McElheran Author:

Publisher: Oxford | No. 95.314 | Price: 75¢

Voicing: SSAATBB | Grade: med. | Time: 3:00

Accompaniment: a cappella

Type of Text: "scat" syllables

Range and Tessitura: relative to individual singer

Avant-garde:

graphic notations of pitch, rhythm; clapping; foot stamping; finger snaps; thigh slaps; tongue clicks; voiced, unvoiced trills; humming; ad libitum use of materials; unmetered time segments

Traditional: not applicable

CANTUS FIRMUS

Composer: Bert Konowitz and Orlando DiGirolamo | Author:

Publisher: Alfred | No. 6173 | Price: 60¢

Voicing: SSA div. | Grade: med-diff. | Time:

Accompaniment: piano;[1] tambourine - optional

Type of Text: scat syllables

Range and Tessitura:

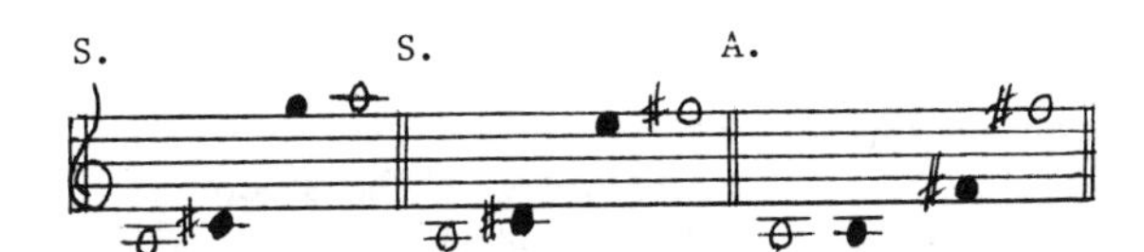


Avant-garde:

ad libitum tempo, entrances, dynamics; glissandos; modification of sound with hands; finger snaps; improvisation in jazz idiom; improvisational speech on text

Traditional:

Melody: tonal, modal; shifting tonalities; chromatics

Harmony: functional; ostinato patterns; chords built in fourths; many triads in second inversion and moving in parallel motion; major seconds between adjacent voices

Rhythm: syncopation

---

[1]Need some facility reading accidentals; no reduction of voice parts

CAUTION TO EVERYBODY, A

Composer: Alvin Epstein Author: Ogden Nash

Publisher: Agape No. DI 201 Price: $1.50

Voicing: 2 speakers[1] Grade: med-easy

Time: 1:30

Accompaniment: human percussionist[2]

Type of Text: novelty, humorous

Range and Tessitura: not applicable

Avant-garde:

inflected rhythmic speech; glissandos, whispering; lip flapping; shouting; fragments of syllables; finger snaps; hand rubs; tongue clicks; clapping; drumming

Traditional:

Rhythm: unmetered (4/4 implied by notation and grouping); triplet halfs, quarters, eighths; combinations of eighths and sixteenths

---

[1]Performed by two speakers or two groups of speakers

[2]Individual or group performs the percussion sounds

CELEBRATE

Composer: Don Tyler Author:

Publisher: Pallma No. Ed. PC 811 Price: 35¢

Voicing: SATB Grade: med-easy Time:

Accompaniment: a cappella

Type of Text: sacred; jubilation

Range and Tessitura:

Avant-garde:

rhythmic speech and singing combined (ranges from whispering to shouting dynamically)

Traditional:

Melody: tonal; modulating

Harmony: functional; open fifths in parallel motion

Rhythm: syncopation; cross rhythms; combinations of eighths and sixteenths

CHANT AND JUBILATION

Composer: Hal H. Hopson Author: Hal H. Hopson

Publisher: Flammer No. D-5228 Price: 35¢

Voicing: SA(T)B Grade: easy Time: 3:20

Accompaniment: organ; snare drum; suspended cymbal

Type of Text: sacred; praise of God

Range and Tessitura:

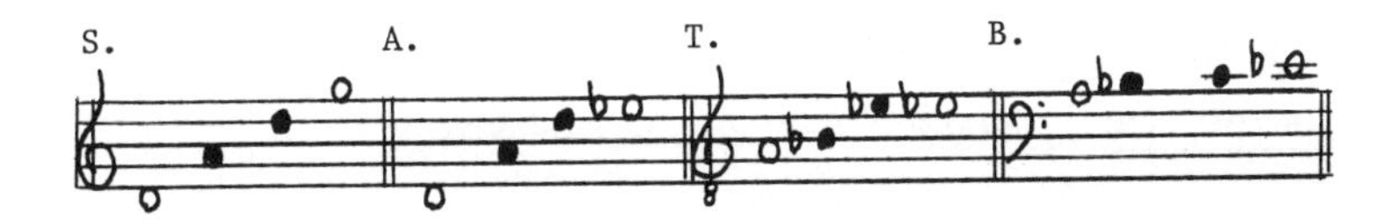

Avant-garde:

rhythmic speech; shouting

Traditional:

Melody: tonal; conjunct

Harmony: functional; parallel thirds, sixths; frequent unisons

Rhythm: triplet quarters; syncopation

CHANT FOR SPIKE MILLIGAN

Composer: Brian Dennis Author: Spike Milligan
Publisher: Universal No. 15454 Price: 35¢
Voicing: three-part Grade: easy Time: 5:00
Accompaniment: instruments which go "BONG," "PING," CLANG"; each speaker should have an instrument
Type of Text: nonsense words
Range and Tessitura: not applicable
Avant-garde:

speaking; ad libitum accents/stresses, entrances, rhythms; shouting

Traditional: not applicable

CHILD'S GHETTO, A

Composer: Hanley Jackson Author:
Publisher: Walton No. 2916 Price: 35¢
Voicing: SATB div. Grade: med. Time: 6:00
Accompaniment: electronic tape[1]
Type of Text: secular; serious; mood-evoking

Range and Tessitura:

Avant-garde:

glissando; tone clusters; ad libitum rhythm, use of text; tongue clicks; murmuring

Traditional:

Melody: nontonal; disjunct; fourths, sevenths; repetition of intervals

Harmony: nonfunctional; dissonant; tape aids in build up of massive dissonant chord; unisons between adjacent voices

Rhythm: unmetered; stop watch needed; triplet quarters

[1]Tape available - $10.00; no reduction of voice parts in score

CHORTOS I

Composer: Richmond Browne Author: biblical

Publisher: Flammer No. A-5629 Price: 30¢

Voicing: speaking chorus Grade: easy Time: 5:00

Accompaniment: a cappella

Type of Text: sacred; Psalm 104, Revelations; the earth, grass, end of world

Range and Tessitura: not applicable

Avant-garde:

ad libitum speaking, singing; noises (coins, keys, paper, etc.); choreography; whistling

Traditional: not applicable

[1]At least 25 voices; mixed or all men; one section for men only

CHRISTMAS COLLAGE

Composer: Carlton Young Author: Carlton Young

Publisher: Agape No. AG 7168 Price: 40¢

Voicing: 2 two-part choirs[1] Grade: easy Time:

Accompaniment: two organs or two electric pianos; wind chimes

Type of Text: sacred; bits of carols

Range and Tessitura:

Avant-garde:

inflected rhythmic speech; ad libitum repetition, choice of coda; moaning; sighs; whistling; special location of choirs

Traditional:

Melody: bits of traditional Christmas carols, all tonal

Harmony: results of rounds or canons; unisons

Rhythm: changing meters (6/8, 6/4, 4/4, 12/4)

[1]Choir #1 sings three four-part chords

CHRISTMAS MUSIC

Composer: Edwin London Author:

Publisher: Agape  No. AG 7161  Price: $1.00
Voicing: SATB; T. solo  Grade: diff[1]  Time: 13:20
Accompaniment: organ; bells; glockenspiel; anything with bell-like tone
Type of Text: secular/sacred; bits of many carols; sarcastic
Range and Tessitura:

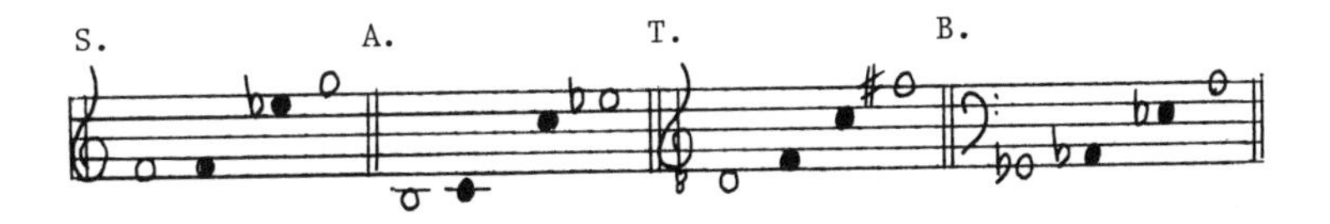


Avant-garde:

improvisation on carols (composer would like each singer to be able to "solo" on a carol of own choice); whispering; ad libitum pitch, talking

Traditional: 30 measures of original music by composer

Melody: tonal, chromatics; conjunct

Harmony: functional; chromatic

Rhythm: syncopation; displaced accents; two-against-three

[1]Level of difficulty for the thirty measures of original music.

CINCO VOCE

Composer: Craig Kupka  Author: Craig Kupka
Publisher: Walton  No. 2919  Price: 35¢
Voicing: six-part chorus[1]  Grade: med-easy  Time:
Accompaniment: trombone,[2] sandblocks
Type of Text: sacred; creation in God

Range and Tessitura:

Avant-garde:

ad libitum tempo, entrances, selection of musical fragments

Traditional:

Melody: tonal; some chromatics

Harmony: aleatoric

Rhythm: unmetered; traditional eighths, quarters, dotted quarters, halfs

---

[1]A drone chorus of five to six singers; other five parts sing independently; minimum of 30 singers, 60 to 90 preferred; each part will need to be learned separately because there is no established rhythm between the parts

[2]Trombonist improvises around the pitch of "D"; no reduction of voice parts (cf. footnote #1)

CIRCLE

Composer: John Carter Author: John Carter

Publisher: Walton No. 2926 Price 60¢

Voicing: mixed chorus Grade: med. Time:

Accompaniment: a cappella

Type of Text: sacred/secular; meaning of circle

Range and Tessitura:

Avant-garde:

approximate pitch; graphic notation of pitch; whispering; rhythmic speech; fragments of words (vowels, consonants); ad libitum use of musical fragments, tempo, entrances

Traditional:

Melody: fragments too short to speak of tonality; major/minor seconds predominate

Harmony: aleatoric

Rhythm: unmetered; traditional symbols used

CLOUD CANTICLE

Composer: Wilfred Mellers Author: Ronald Johnson

Publisher: Galliard No. 26043 Price:

Voicing: SATB double choir;[1] ST solo Grade: diff. Time:

Accompaniment: a cappella[2]

Type of Text: secular; moods

Range and Tessitura:

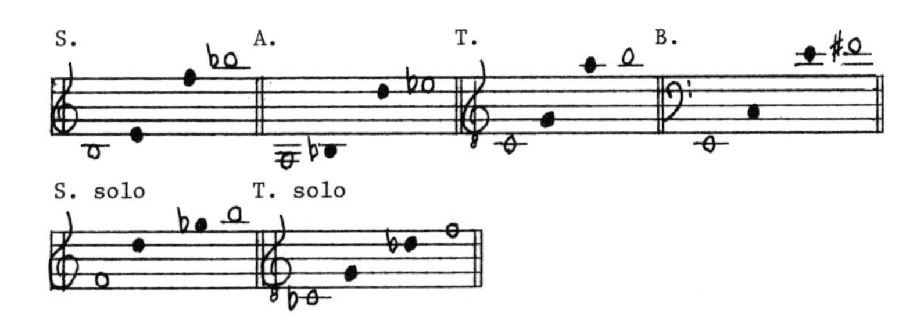

Avant-garde:

tone clusters; graphic notation of pitch, rhythm; improvisation on supplied pitches; ad libitum rhythm, tempo; cries; yells; glissandos

Traditional:

Melody: nontonal; chromatic; chord patterns; major/minor seconds

Harmony: nonfunctional; major/minor seconds between adjacent voices; at times the two choirs double each other, other times sing a second apart

Rhythm: changing meters (5/8, 6/8, 2/4, 7/8, 8/8, 3/4, 5/16+3/8, 5/16+1/4, 5/4, 9/8, 6/4, 5/16+5/8, 1/4, 4/4); unmetered sections; triplet eighths; two-against-three, three-against-five; syncopation; combinations of eighths and sixteenths; five eighths to a beat

[1]Each choir also divisi; probably would have to rehearse each choir separately

[2]No reduction of voice parts

COLLAGE

Composer: Alvin Epstein Author:

Publisher: Agape No. AG 7150 Price: 40¢

Voicing: SATB[1] Grade: diff. Time:

Accompaniment: violin; double bass; horn; cello; clarinet; oboe; bassoon[2]

Type of Text: sacred; Kyrie; nonsense syllables (work might be considered a "serious" novelty rather than religious)

Range and Tessitura:

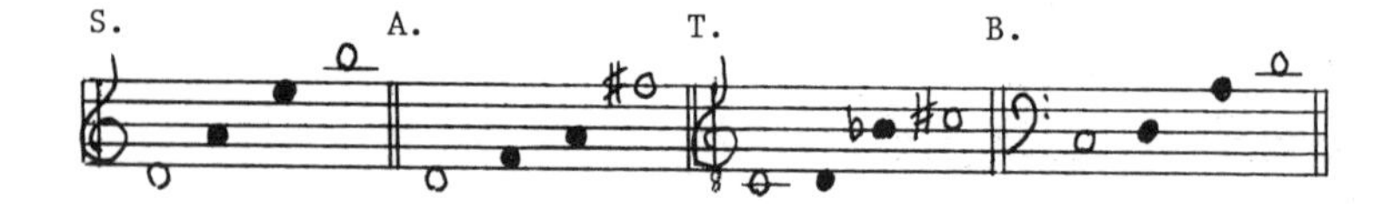

Avant-garde:

ad libitum entrances, pitch, rhythm; graphic notation of pitch; finger snaps; clapping; lip flapping; tone clusters; cluster glissandos; rhythmic speech shouting; choreography for entrances

Traditional:

Melody: Gregorian chants; nontonal; chromatics

Harmony: generally aleatoric; other is nonfunctional

Rhythm: unmetered throughout; free chant rhythm; traditional rhythmic symbols used in ad libitum parts

---

[1]Solo voices drawn from each section; final chord divisi

[2]No reduction of voice parts; instrumentalists need facility

COLLECT

Composer: Leslie Bassett  Author: Anon

Publisher: Westwood  No. CA-2000-8  Price:

Voicing: SATB div.  Grade: diff.  Time: 4:00

Accompaniment: electronic tape[1]

Type of Text: sacred; penitential

Range and Tessitura:

Avant-garde:

choir's music totally traditional in notation, sound; sing with electronic tape sounds (tape cues pitches for choir also)

Traditional:

Melody: very disjunct; augmented, diminished intervals; chromatic

Harmony: nonfunctional; chords built on fourths; no tonal feeling in usual sense

Rhythm: changing meters (5/4, 4/4, 3/4, 2/4, 7/8, 6/8, 5/8); syncopation; triplet quarters

[1]No reduction of voice parts

COMRADE! BROTHER!

Composer: Jack Boyd    Author: Stephen Crane

Publisher: G. Schirmer    No. 11510    Price: 25¢

Voicing: SATB[1]    Grade: med.    Time:

Accompaniment: a cappella

Type of Text: secular/sacred; devil is man's brother

Range and Tessitura:

Avant-garde:

glissandos; speaking voice at ends of words; prolongation of consonant sounds in words

Traditional:

Melody: tonal; disjunct; chordal patterns; repetition of melodic patterns

Harmony: functional; repetition of patterns; open fourths, fifths; unisons

Rhythm: changing meters (4/4, 3/4); combinations of eighths and sixteenths; syncopation

[1]Soprano has three divisi chords

COSMIC FESTIVAL

Composer: Richard Felciano  Author: several[1]

Publisher: E. C. Schirmer  No. 2938  Price:

Voicing: Unison  Grade: easy  Time: 6:00

Accompaniment: electronic tape

Type of Text: secular/sacred; praise of life, man, earth

Range and Tessitura:

Avant-garde:

music cells according to a scheme; everything traditional in notation and sound; sing with electronic tape sounds

Traditional:

Melody: modal; scale and chordal patterns

Harmony: not applicable

Rhythm: syncopation

[1]Walt Whitman; Elizabeth Barrett Browning; Ralph Waldo Emerson

CRADLE HYMN AND HODIE[1]

Composer: Hanley Jackson  Author: biblical

Publisher: Shawnee No. A 1319 Price: 50¢

Voicing: SATB div.; 2 narrators Grade: diff. Time: 2:30-3:00

Accompaniment: electronic tape[2]

Type of Text: sacred; Christmas; Latin[3]

Range and Tessitura:

Avant-garde:

rhythmic speech; rhythmic speech and singing combined; whispering; tone clusters; ad libitum alternation of vowels, repetition of text; glissandos; wide vibrato

Traditional:

Melody: 1) tonal, chromatics; 2) tonality obscure; ostinatos; disjunct

Harmony: 1) functional; sevenths; major/minor seconds between adjacent voices; chords composed of two triads a second apart 2) nonfunctional; ostinatos give functional effect; fourths, modified fifths; major/minor seconds between adjacent voices

Rhythm: changing meters (4/4, 3/4, 5/4); syncopation

---

[1]Two movements; can be performed separately

[2]Tape available - $6.00 (stereo)

[3]Latin text sung by choir; narrators use English text

CREATE AND CELEBRATE

Composer: F. Dale Bengtson Author:

Publisher: Gentry No. G-205 Price: 30¢

Voicing: two-part speaking chorus Grade: easy Time:

Accompaniment: optional maracas, claves, tom-tom

Type of Text: secular (could be considered sacred); celebration of man and his senses

Range and Tessitura: not applicable

Avant-garde:

inflected rhythmic speech; voiced trilled glissando; modification of sound with hands; ad libitum use of text; conductor's ad libitum dynamics, entrances

Traditional:

Rhythm: syncopation

CREATION, THE

Composer: Michael Hennagin Author: biblical; James Joyce

Publisher: Walton No. 2186 Price: $1.00

Voicing: SATB; SAB solos[1] Grade: med. Time:

Accompaniment: 3 sets brass wind-bells; 3 educator bells; alto recorder; suspended cymbal; large gong; chimes; orchestra bells; piano; marimba; electronic tape - optional[2]

Type of Text: sacred; creation of light, man

Range and Tessitura:

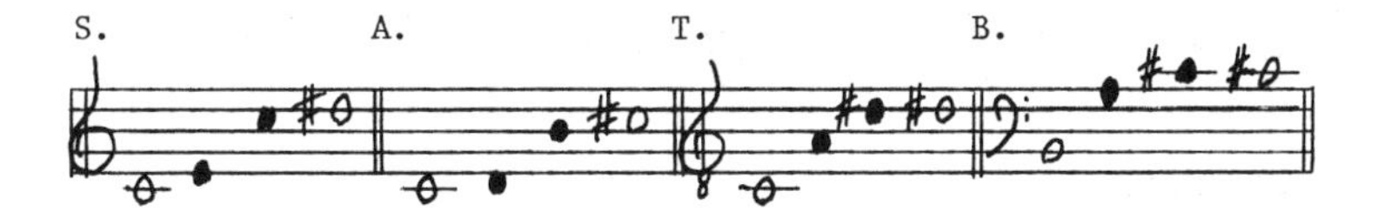


Avant-garde:

inflected rhythmic speech; glissandos; graphic notation of pitch; whispering; shouting; tongue clicks; choreography

Traditional:

Melody: rhythmic chanting on pitch; snatches of tonal melody; disjunct; chromatic; conjunct

Harmony: nonfunctional; major seconds between adjacent voices; fifths

Rhythm: changing meters (6/4, 4/4, 2/4); unmetered; triplet eighths; three-against-two; triplet quarters for soloists

---

[1] Four each; each section chants on single pitch; divisi rhythmically; unison rhythmic speech

[2] Tape - $10. 00; includes cues for complete work: The Family of Man

CREDO

Composer: Robert Berglund Author: Florence Johnson

Publisher: Beacon Hill No. AN-6021 Price: 60¢

Voicing: SATB div. Grade: med. Time:

Accompaniment: a cappella

Type of Text: sacred; setting of John 9 (curing of blind man)

Range and Tessitura:

Avant-garde:

rhythmic speech; glissandos

Traditional:

Melody: tonal, modal; some chromaticism; few augmented, diminished intervals

Harmony: mostly functional; many sevenths, ninths; chords with added tones; parallel fourths, fifths; major/minor seconds between adjacent voices; unison, two-part passages

Rhythm: one unmetered section; syncopation prominant; unison, two-part rhythmic movement

CRY OUT AND SHOUT

Composer: Ben Ludlow    Author: biblical

Publisher: Flammer    No. A-5628    Price: 30¢

Voicing: SATB, speech choir    Grade: easy    Time: 1:30

Accompaniment: snare drum[1]

Type of Text: sacred; Isaiah 12:6; praise

Range and Tessitura: not applicable

Avant-garde:

rhythmic speech

Traditional:

Rhythm: syncopation; triplet quarters, eighths

[1]Part supplied with vocal score

CURSE THE SOURCE OF DELIGHT

Composer: Gordon Johnson    Author: Elizabeth Wrancher

Publisher: Marks    No. MC 4593    Price: 50¢

Voicing: SATB div.    Grade: med.    Time: 2:10

Accompaniment: piano; timpani; tom-tom

Type of Text: secular; serious; nonsense words chanted

Range and Tessitura:

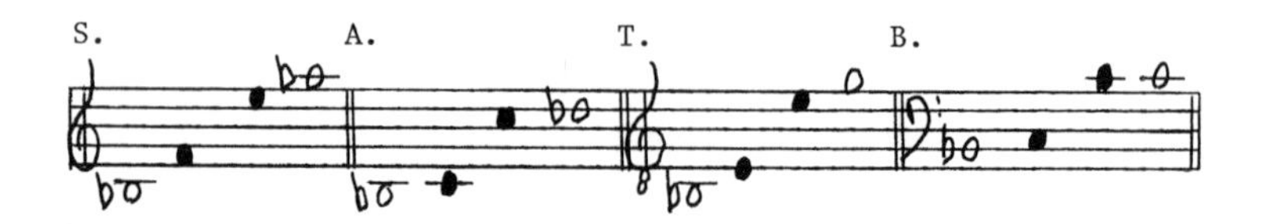


Avant-garde:

inflected rhythmic speech; sustained "s"; approximate notation of pitch

Traditional:

Melody: tonal, modal; ostinatos

Harmony: built in fourths, fifths; unisons for SA, TB

Rhythm: fast sixteenths; triplet eighths; syncopation

DANIEL IN THE LION'S DEN

Composer: Daniel Pinkham Author: biblical[1]

Publisher: E. C. Schirmer No. 2946 Price:

Voicing: SATB div; T, B, B solos[2] Grade: diff. Time:

Accompaniment: two pianos; timpani; glockenspiel; triangle; woodblock; tambourine; suspended cymbal; crash cymbals; giant tam-tam; snare drum; 3 tom-toms; base drum; electronic tape[3]

Type of Text: sacred; story of the title

Range and Tessitura:

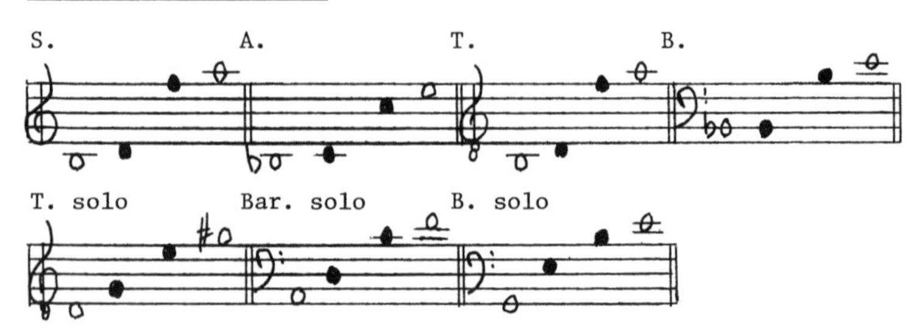

Avant-garde:

ad libitum performance of supplied music cells; graphic notation of pitch; modification of sound with hands; growls; roars; shouts; glissandos

Traditional:

Melody: chromatic; occasionally disjunct

Harmony: nonfunctional; ostinatos, repetitions of progressions; augmented, diminished chords

Rhythm: changing meters (4/4, 2/4, 5/8, 7/8, 3/8, 5/4, 6/8); unmetered section; polymeters in aleatoric section, otherwise parts move in rhythmic unison; syncopation

---

[1]Poem by John Newton

[2]Solo parts very difficult, chromatic, a cappella, nontonal, disjunct

[3]Pianist must be very skilled; other instrumentalists need good technique and rhythmic sense

DAY OF DESOLATION

Composer: Edwin London Author: biblical

Publisher: Boonin No. 131 Price: $1.25

Voicing: SATB div.; 4 S. 1T. solo 2 speakers Grade: diff. Time:

Accompaniment: bells

Type of Text: sacred; Isaiah 10:3; "judgment day" or "end of the world"

Range and Tessitura:

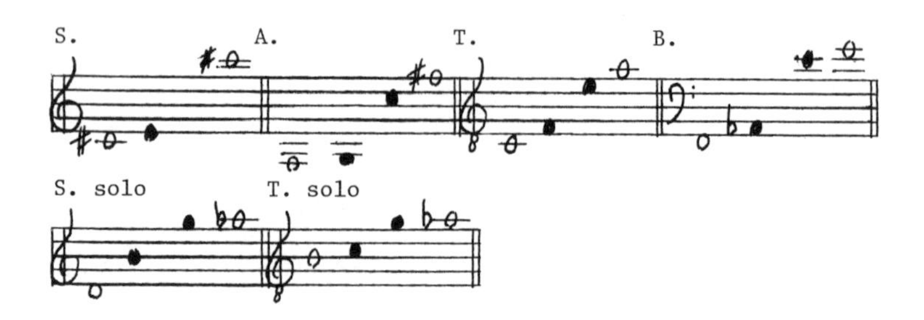


Avant-garde:

graphic notation of rhythm; ad libitum pitch, rhythm; glissandos; screaming; quarter tones; inflected rhythmic speech

Traditional:

Melody: nontonal; chromatic; disjunct; augmented, diminished octaves frequent

Harmony: nonfunctional; major/minor seconds between adjacent voices; augmented and diminished octaves sounded together

Rhythm: changing meters (6/4, 9/4, 5/4, 3/16, 4/4); cross rhythms; triplet quarters, eighths; smaller divisions of beat; polyrhythms

## DAY OF PENTECOST[1]

Composer: Leland B. Sateren Author: Thomas W. Wersell

Publisher: Augsburg No. 11-3501 Price: 60¢

Voicing: SATB div. Grade: med-diff. Time:

Accompaniment: a cappella[2]

Type of Text: sacred; events of Pentecost of New Testament; liturgical

Range and Tessitura:

Avant-garde:

ad libitum rhythm, tempo, dynamics; glissandos; graphic notation of pitch; inflected rhythmic speech; tone clusters; whispering; improvisation on text; rhythmic speech and singing combined

Traditional:

Melody: tonal; shifting tonality; chromatics; Gregorian chant melodies; shift from chant to more modern style of melody

Harmony: functional; sevenths; parallel fifths; major/minor seconds between adjacent voices

Rhythm: changing meters (2/4, 4/4, 3/2, 3/4); unmetered sections; free rhythm of chant; syncopation; combinations of eighths and sixteenths

---

[1]Work of five movements; liturgical; can be performed separately

[2]No reduction of voice parts

DE PROFUNDIS

Composer: Knut Nystedt    Author: biblical

Publisher: AMP    No. A-499    Price: 40¢

Voicing: SSATB div.; T. solo[1]    Grade: diff.    Time: 8:30

Accompaniment: a cappella[2]

Type of Text: sacred; Psalm 130; penitential

Range and Tessitura:

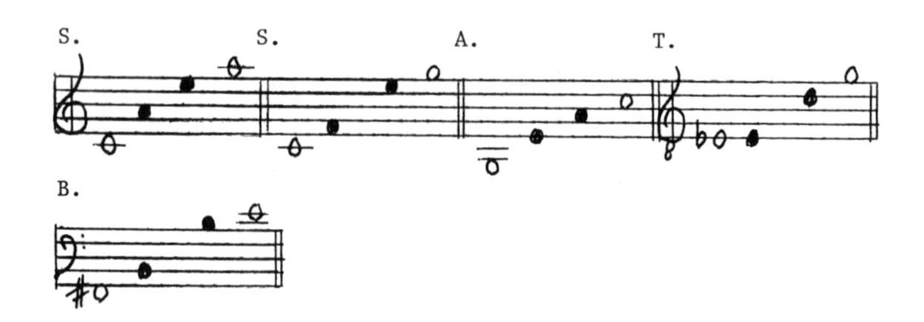


Avant-garde:

tone clusters; cluster glissandos; graphic notation of melody

Traditional:

Melody: rhythmic chanting on one pitch; much half-step, whole step motion; diminished, augmented intervals

Harmony: nonfunctional; building of ostinato chords; major/minor seconds between adjacent voices; fourths; augmented and diminished chords; close voicing

Rhythm: changing meters (6/2, 3/2, 4/2, 2/2); unmetered; triplet eighths; three-against-two

---

[1]Tenor solo of twenty beats; chant intonation of "Gloria"

[2]No reduction of voice parts

DE PROFUNDIS

Composer: Arnold Schoenberg Author: biblical

Publisher: MCA No. 11193-062 Price: $1.25

Voicing: SSATBB; S. solo[1] Grade: diff. Time: 5:00

Accompaniment: a cappella

Type of Text: sacred; Psalm 130; penitential

Range and Tessitura:

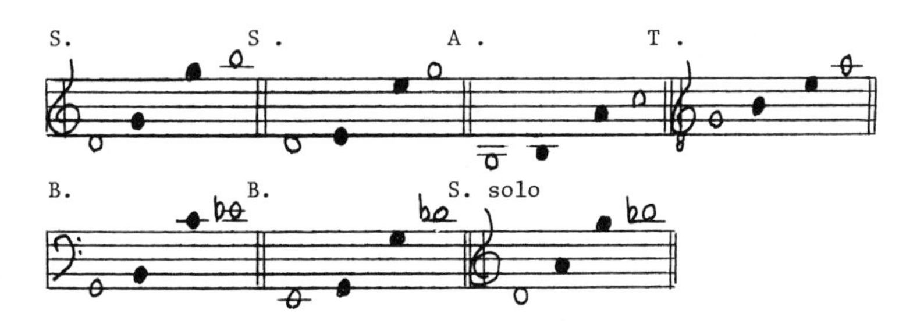


Avant-garde:

inflected rhythmic speech

Traditional: built on a hexachord series

Melody: disjunct; chromatic; augmented, diminished intervals

Harmony: nonfunctional; augmented, diminished chords; fourths, fifths, ninths between adjacent voices

Rhythm: polyrhythm; triplet eighths; syncopation; three-against-four

[1]Soprano solo of six measures

DESCENT OF THE CELESTIAL CITY, THE

Composer: Iain Hamilton | Author: biblical

Publisher: Presser | No. 312-41004 | Price: 45¢

Voicing: SATB div[1] | Grade: med. | Time:

Accompaniment: organ[2]

Type of Text: sacred; Revelations; heavenly Jerusalem

Range and Tessitura:[3]

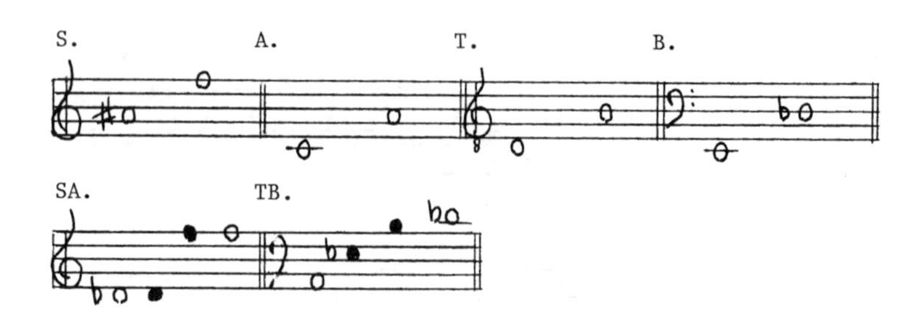


Avant-garde:

rhythmic speech; tone cluster written out (built by adding one pitch at a time)

Traditional:

Melody: (small choir) nontonal; disjunct intervals but much recitation on same pitch

Harmony: (small choir) all unison passages

Rhythm: changing meters (4/4, 3/4, 5/4, 2/4, 6/4); triplet eighths, sixteenths; combinations of eighths and sixteenths

---

[1]Principal choir divided into six written parts for each section to build tone cluster; small choir SATB to function as "solo" group

[2]Organ independent of choral parts in rhythmic speech sections; supplies pitch cues in building tone cluster; organist must be able to read accidentals, have good rhythmic sense

[3]Range of tone cluster, only sung part for principal choir

DIALOGUE

Composer: Robert Karlén Author: biblical; Kierkegaard

Publisher: AMSI No. AMS 175 Price:

Voicing: SATB div. Grade: diff. Time:

Accompaniment: a cappella; electronic tape[1]

Type of Text: sacred; God's unchangeableness; man's rest in God

Range and Tessitura:

Avant-garde:

rhythmic speech; clapping; tone clusters;[2] singing and speaking combined

Traditional:

Melody: tonal, chromatic; shifting tonality; some disjunct intervals

Harmony: frequently nonfunctional; polytonality; open fifths, octaves; unisons; parallel seconds between adjacent voices; altered chords of every description

Rhythm: changing meters (2/4, 3/4, 4/4); triplet quarters; three-against-four; choir moves at half the speed of the taped choir

---

[1]Tape made by choir singing music composed to biblical text; choir then sings with playback of tape music composed to Kierkegaard text

[2]Cluster formed by singers singing from pitch to pitch (a fifth) ad libitum, creating a cluster with "internal motion"

DIGRESSIONS

Composer: Barry Vercoe Author: Toyohiko Kagawa[1]

Publisher: Elkan-Vogel No. Price: $2.50[2]

Voicing: SATB/SATB[3] Grade: diff. Time: 15:00

Accompaniment: electronic tape; piano; optional orchestral accompaniment[4]

Type of Text: sacred/secular; earth a "victim" of man

Range and Tessitura:

Avant-garde:

song-speech; glissando; whispering; rhythmic speech; approximate notation of pitch

Traditional:

Melody: Gregorian chants; nontonal; each choir own key; chromatic; disjunct at times

Harmony: nonfunctional; major/minor seconds between adjacent voices; unison for two or more voices; altered chords

Rhythm: changing meters (4/4, 5/4, 7/8, 5/8, 6/4); unmetered; triplet eighths, quarters; two-against-three; three-against-four; syncopation; combinations of eighths and sixteenths

---

[1]Other texts from the Latin Liturgy

[2]Tape - $2. 50; orchestra parts - $60. 00

[3]Each choir has own text; suggested each rehearse separately to assure independence

[4]No reduction of voice parts

DIVISION

Composer: Samuel Adler  Author: W. S. Merwin
Publisher: Agape  No. AG 7126  Price: 75¢
Voicing: TTBB, six-part speaking choir[1]  Grade: diff.  Time:
Accompaniment: glockenspiel[2]
Type of Text: sacred/secular; division, unity among men
Range and Tessitura:[3]

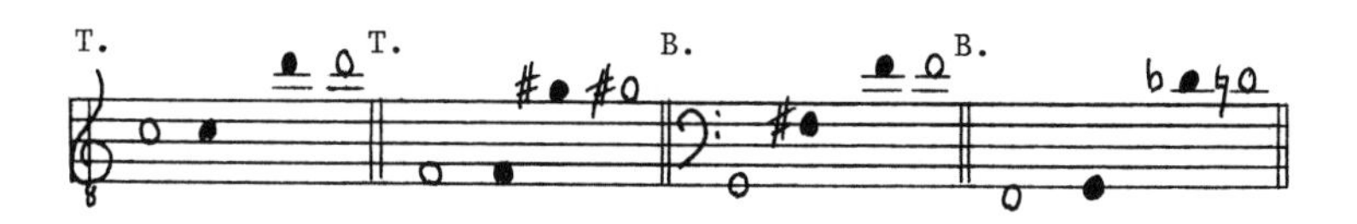


Avant-garde:

written out tone clusters; rhythmic speech; whispering; ad libitum pitch, tempo; falsetto; inflected rhythmic speech

Traditional:

Melody: nontonal; ostinato melodic patterns; cross voices; chromatics; conjunct, disjunct

Harmony: functional feeling through repetition of patterns; close voicing; major/minor seconds between adjacent voices

Rhythm: changing meters (4/4, 3/4, 6/8, 7/8, 5/8); combinations of eighths and sixteenths; triplet eighths, quarters, sixteenths; three-against-four; (six speaking parts have strongly independent lines rhythmically); syncopation

---

[1]Can be performed SATB also

[2]No reduction of voice parts for speech choir; piano reduction of singing choir for rehearsal; performer on glockenspiel needs facility

[3]Composer specifies that some pitches be sung falsetto

DO YOU WANT HIM?

Composer: John Stanley Author: N. C. Habel

Publisher: New Music No. NMA-119 Price: 35¢

Voicing: SATB div.; T. solo Grade: med-easy Time:

Accompaniment: a cappella[1]

Type of Text: sacred; acceptance of Christ?

Range and Tessitura:

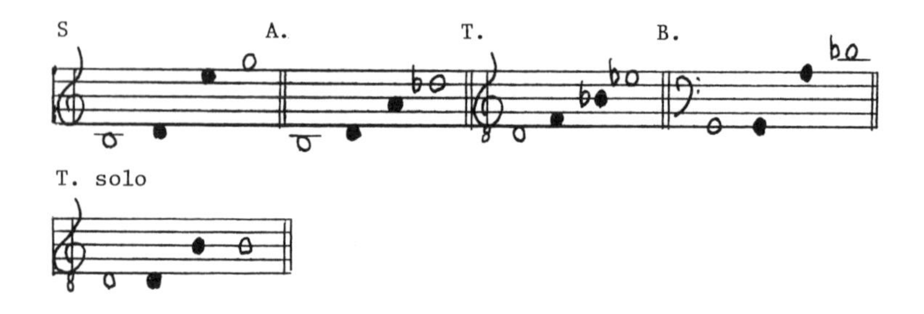


Avant-garde:

rhythmic speech; glissandos; tone clusters; ad libitum speaking of text; whispering; nontraditional rhythmic notation for unmetered sections

Traditional:

Melody: ostinato phrases; some chromaticism with a model feeling

Harmony: nonfunctional, but ostinato progressions give functional feel; open fifths, fourths between adjacent voices; altered chords

Rhythm: unmetered sections (with nontraditional notation); triplet quarters; syncopation

[1]No reduction of voice parts

DOGS, COFFEE, AND ALLIGATORS[1]

Composer: Donald E. Matthews Author: D. E. Matthews
Publisher: General No. Ed. GC 37 Price: 35¢
Voicing: SATB[2] Grade: med. Time:
Accompaniment: a cappella
Type of Text: secular; novelty
Range and Tessitura:

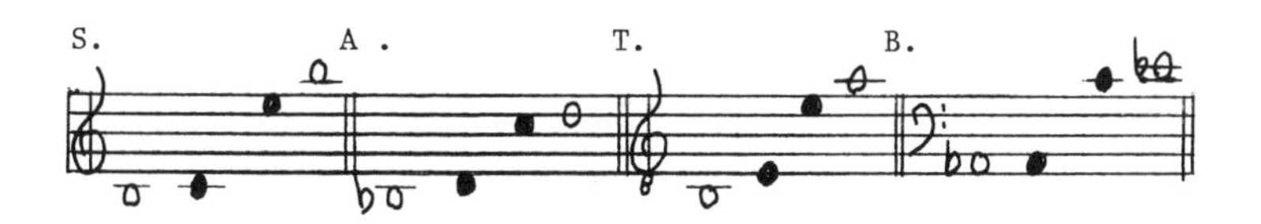


Avant-garde:

glissandos; rhythmic speech; screams; barking; facial choreography

Traditional:

Melody: modal, chromatic; scale, chordal patterns; ostinatos

Harmony: modal; functional; unison, two-part passages

Rhythm: syncopation

---

[1]Three compositions and an interlude

[2]Bass - two measures of divisi

DOWN A DIFFERENT ROAD[1]

Composer: Brent Pierce Author:
Publisher: Walton No. 2915 Price: 50¢
Voicing: SATB[2] Grade: med-easy Time:
Accompaniment: coke bottles; piano;[3] brass wind chimes; pail of water

Type of Text: secular; novelty; syllables; vowels; city names

Range and Tessitura:

Avant-garde:

graphic notation of pitch, rhythm; rhythmic speaking; tongue clicks; whispering; murmuring; flutter tongue; sighing; clapping; glissandos; ad libitum whispering; tone clusters

Traditional:

Melody: tonal, modal; canons; pedal points

Harmony: tonal; written out tone clusters; ostinatos

Rhythm: unmetered section; syncopation

---

[1]Three movement suite; can be performed separately

[2]Notated for two high, two low voices; also high, medium, low

[3]Pianist needs some facility for part in third movement

DREAM

Composer: Arne Mellnäs Author: e. e. cummings

Publisher: Hansen No. WH 101 Price:

Voicing: SATB div. Grade: diff. Time:

Accompaniment: a cappella

Type of Text: secular; dream objects

Range and Tessitura:[1]

Avant-garde:

tone clusters; glissandos; prolongations of consonants of words

Traditional:

Melody: nontonal; chromatics; major/minor seconds prominant; some disjunct passages

Harmony: nonfunctional; major/minor seconds between adjacent voices

Rhythm: unmetered throughout; divisi parts sing same melodic fragment in two different note values (e.g.: tenor I sings all notes as half-note values while tenor II sings same pitches as dotted-half-note values); triplet eighths; combinations of eighths and sixteenths

[1]Tone clusters extend beyond the range of the specified pitches

DREAM SONG

Composer: Paul Chihara Author:

Publisher: Elkan-Vogel No. 362-03176 Price: 40¢

Voicing: SATB div. Grade: diff. Time: 3:00

Accompaniment: a cappella[1]

Type of Text: secular; syllables (oh, doh, wah, yah)

Range and Tessitura:

Avant-garde:

glissandos

Traditional:

Melody: little traditional melody; long sustained notes; ostinato figures; many glissandos

Harmony: nonfunctional: parallel thirds between adjacent voices; augmented, diminished intervals; sevenths, ninths; added tones

Rhythm: changing meters (4/4, 3/4, 2/4); syncopation; triplet quarters, halfs; three-against-two; cross rhythms

---

[1]No reduction of voice parts

DREAM THING ON BIBLICAL EPISODES

Composer: Edwin London   Author: biblical

Publisher: Agape   No. AG 7162   Price: $1.00

Voicing: SSAA div.,[1] soloists[2]   Grade: diff.   Time:

Accompaniment: a cappella[3]

Type of Text: sacred; lamenting, questioning, consoling

Range and Tessitura:

Avant-garde:

glissandos; whispering; vibrato; screams; rolled "R"; finger snaps; ad libitum use of pitches, rhythms

Traditional:

Melody: nontonal; disjunct; chromatic; augmented, diminished intervals of every type; probably each part will have to be practiced independently

Harmony: nonfunctional; seconds, sevenths, augmented, diminished chords of every type

Rhythm: unmetered sections; changing meters (4/4, 12/8, 3/4, 2/4, 9/16, 5/8); triplet halfs, quarters, eighths, sixteenths; combinations of eighths and sixteenths

---

[1]Composer advises shifting voices to achieve proper balance in the various sections, even if it means altos are to sing with 2nd sopranos

[2]Six solo voices are needed in one section; at other times the number ranges from one to four; two soloists need a high C#; soloists improvise on supplied pitches; range of the particular solo part will determine the type of voice to be used

[3]No reduction of voice parts

EARTH'S A BAKED APPLE, THE

Composer: Michael Colgrass Author: Michael Colgrass

Publisher: MCA No. 18360-044 Price: $3.00

Voicing: SATB, boy soprano[1] Grade: diff. Time: 11:00

Accompaniment: two options: 1) small ensemble - clarinet, trumpet, trombone, contrabass, piano, percussion; 2) orchestra - 3 clarinets, contrabassoon, 4 horns, 3 trumpets, tuba, harp, piano, celesta, 5 percussion, strings, jazz band

Type of Text: secular; youth spirit; syllables, vowels, consonants

Range and Tessitura:

Avant-garde:

graphic notation of pitch, rhythm; glissandos; inflected rhythmic speech; rhythmic speech, ad libitum pitch; audible inhale, exhale; tongue clicks; tongue flapping; whispering; screaming, shouting, calling (to create pandemonium)

Traditional:

Melody: tonal; shifting tonality; repeated figures; disjunct; chromatic; cross voices; outlines of seventh chords

Harmony: nonfunctional; altered chords; sevenths; unison, two-part passages; sevenths, diminished octaves between adjacent voices

Rhythm: changing meters (4/4, 3/4, 2/4, 3/8); syncopation; triplet eighths, sixteenths; combinations of eighths and sixteenths

[1]Various combinations of "solos" drawn from each section; boy soprano part can be performed by woman: difficult line, disjunct, chromatic

EASTER CAROL: NOW IS THE HOUR OF DARKNESS PAST

Composer: Daniel Pinkham Author:

Publisher: E. C. Schirmer No. 2955 Price:

Voicing: SATB[1] Grade: med. Time:

Accompaniment: electronic tape; triangle - optional

Type of Text: sacred; Easter alleluia

Range and Tessitura:

Avant-garde:

choral parts are totally traditional in notation; perform with electronic tape

Traditional:

Melody: tonal, modal; scale and chordal patterns prominant; repetition of melodic passages

Harmony: functional; major seconds between adjacent voices; open fifths; many three part passages (SAT or SA, T, B)

Rhythm: much unison rhythmic movement

---

[1]Two chords require SA divisi; six-part chord ends piece

[2]At times voice parts use open score; tape available; optional percussion parts available

## EIGHTEEN MOVEMENTS[1]

Composer: Eskil Hemberg Author:

Publisher: Hansen No. WH - 123 Price: $2.00

Voicing: SATB div.[2] Grade: easy to med-diff. Time: 20:00

Accompaniment: a cappella; projections - optional[3]

Type of Text: secular; nursery rhymes

Range and Tessitura:

Avant-garde:

inflected rhythmic speech; rhythmic speech and singing combined; tone clusters; approximate pitch, rhythm; graphic notation of rhythm; ad libitum rhythm; choreography[4]

Traditional:

Melody: tonal; shifting tonality; bitonal; chromatics; conjunct, disjunct intervals; variety because of number movements

Harmony: functional; bitonal; close voicings; open fifths; parallel thirds; major/minor seconds between adjacent voices; unisons, octave doublings; variety because of number of movements

Rhythm: each movement has own meter; changing meter within a movement (6/8, 3/4; alternating measures of 12/8, 9/8); combinations of eighths and sixteenths; triplet eighths; much unison rhythmic movement; three-against-two

---

[1]Eighteen short movements; can perform in any combination

[2]Scored for diverse voicing from large mixed choir to solo voice

[3]Illustrations of nursery rhymes available

[4]Choreography by Thor Zachrisson - optional; can create own also

EM

Composer: Victor Hoyland
Author:
Publisher: Universal
No. 15471
Price: 65¢
Voicing: 24 voices[1]
Grade: med-easy
Time:

Accompaniment: a cappella

Type of Text: vowels and consonants

Range and Tessitura: not applicable

Avant-garde:

whispering; unvoiced sounds; falsetto; moaning; glissandos; graphic notation and ad libitum pitch, rhythm; audible breathing

Traditional: not applicable

[1]Two voices on twelve different parts

EMBODIED WORD, THE

Composer: Walter L. Pelz
Author: C. A. Pennington
Publisher: Augsburg
No. 11-9180
Price: $2.00[1]
Voicing: SATB/SSA, narrator
Grade: med.
Time: 20-25:00

Accompaniment: flute; piano; organ; vibraphone; finger and suspended cymbals; gong; glockenspiel; timpani[2]

Type of Text: sacred; reflections on birth of Christ

Range and Tessitura:

Avant-garde:

glissandos; graphic notation of pitch; improvisation of melodic, rhythmic patterns; inflected rhythmic speech and singing combined; ad libitum use of text; speaking

Traditional:

Melody: tonal; modal; chromatic; conjunct; chordal patterns

Harmony: functional; sevenths, ninths prominant; altered chords, added tones

Rhythm: changing meters (4/4, 2/4, 5/4, 3/4, 6/8, 7/8, 11/8, 5/8, 9/8, 3/2); syncopation; unmetered sections; triplet eighths, quarters; two-against-three

---

[1]Instrumental score available (#11-9182)

[2]Instrumentalists need some facility; two percussionists needed

EPITAPH FOR THIS WORLD AND TIME

Composer: Iain Hamilton Author: biblical

Publisher: Presser No. 412-41057 Price: $4:00

Voicing: 3-SATB choirs, Grade: diff. Time: 22:00

Accompaniment: three organs[2]

Type of Text: sacred; Revelations (Seven Plagues, Fall of Babylon; End of World, Descent of Celestial City)

Range and Tessitura:

Avant-garde:

inflicted rhythmic speech; rhythmic speech; rhythmic speech and singing combined; glissandos; tone clusters written out

Traditional:

Melody: nontonal; chromatic; disjunct; isolated single pitches (pitches generally present in accompaniment); augmented and diminished intervals of every type

Harmony: nonfunctional; major/minor seconds between adjacent voices; altered chords, added tones, construction of chords greatly varied; occasionally two or three choirs sing same lines

Rhythm: changing meters (4/4, 3/4, 5/4, 2/4, 6/4; at times every measure or so a different meter); syncopation; many entrances on parts of beats; triplet quarters, eighths; combinations of eighths and sixteenths; two or three choirs occasionally in rhythmic unison

---

[1]In one passage Choir III SATB with six sub-sections in each part to form written out tone clusters; choirs will probably have to practice parts independently, then put together

[2]No reduction of voice parts; all three organists need facility; important organ interludes throughout composition

ETERNAL VOICES

Composer: Thomas Janson Author: biblical

Publisher: Gray No. GCCS 23 Price: 35¢

Voicing: SATB div. soprano solo Grade: diff. Time:

Accompaniment: a cappella[1]

Type of Text: sacred; Latin (English translation supplied); injunction to faithfulness

Range and Tessitura:

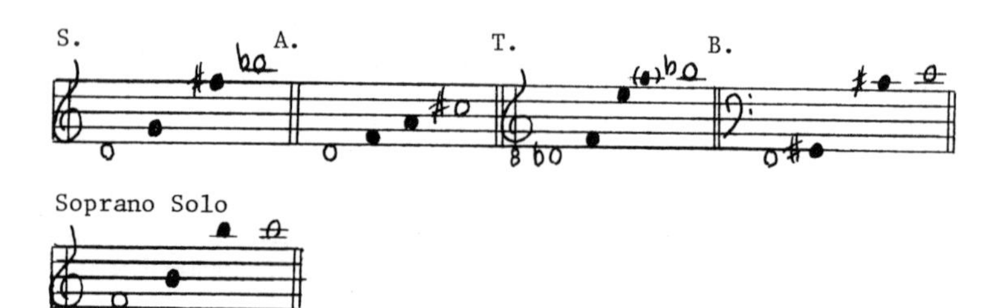


Avant-garde:

ad libitum repetition of pitch in musical fragment, rhythm, tempo; cluster effect, though pitches written out

Traditional:

Melody: nontonal; repetition of melodic patterns; chromatic; disjunct

Harmony: nonfunctional; chords built in fourths and seconds; build up of chords by adding tones; close voicing between four upper voices, also between four lower voices; altered chords common

Rhythm: changing meters (2/4, 3/4, 4/4); unmetered sections; syncopation

---

[1]Solo difficult, nontonal, disjunct, chromatic

[2]No reduction of voice parts

ETUDE AND PATTERN[1]

Composer: Brook McElheran Author:

Publisher: Oxford No. 95.305 Price: 60¢

Voicing: SSAATBB Grade: med. Time: 3:00

Accompaniment: a cappella

Type of Text: secular; syllables, consonants; singers supply own

Range and Tessitura: relative to singer

Avant-garde:

voiced, unvoiced trills; graphic notation of pitch, rhythm; unmetered; ad libitum speaking; humming

Traditional: not applicable

[1]Second movement of a four-movement work; can be performed separately

ETUDE AND SCHERZO[1]

Composer: Brock McElheran Author:

Publisher: Oxford No. 95.307 Price: 50¢

Voicing: SSAATBB Grade: med. Time: 3:00

Accompaniment: a cappella

Type of Text: secular; skat syllables

Range and Tessitura: relative to singer

Avant-garde:

graphic notation of pitch, rhythm; unmetered; ad libitum pitch, rhythm, use of text

Traditional: not applicable

[1]Third movement of a four-movement work; can be performed separately

ETUDE AND SOUNDS[1]

Composer: Brock McElheran Author:

Publisher: Oxford No. 95.313 Price: 50¢

Voicing: SSAATBB Grade: med. Time: 3:00

Accompaniment: a cappella

Type of Text: no text; percussive sound performed by choir

Range and Tessitura: not applicable

Avant-garde:

clapping; foot stamping; finger snaps; thigh slaps; graphic notation of rhythm; unmetered

Traditional: not applicable

[1]First movement of a four-movement work; can be performed separately

EVENING DRAWS IN, THE

Composer: George Self | Author: J. Beckett[1]

Publisher: Universal | No. UE 15423 | Price: 50¢

Voicing: three-part; soloist[2] | Grade: easy | Time: 3:00

Accompaniment: piano (three performers); chime bars; optional metallophones

Type of Text: secular; mood-evoking

Range and Tessitura:

Soloist

Avant-garde:

graphic notation of pitch, rhythm; ad libitum entrances, pitches; unconventional use of piano; speaking

Traditional: only soloist and instrumentalists perform traditionally notated music

Melody: disjunct; augmented, diminished intervals (six pitches in all)

Rhythm: unmetered; graphically notated

[1]Editor of The Keen Edge, source of text

[2]Soloist performs spoken and sung parts; no specification concerning voice type; part rated med-easy

EXULTET CAELUM LAUDIBUS

Composer: John Paynter    Author: 15th-century source

Publisher: Oxford    No. 84.168    Price: 30¢

Voicing: SATB div., S. T. solo    Grade: diff.    Time:

Accompaniment: a cappella; optional glockenspiels; chime bars; metallophones; tubular bells

Type of Text: sacred; Christmas (in English despite title)

Range and Tessitura:

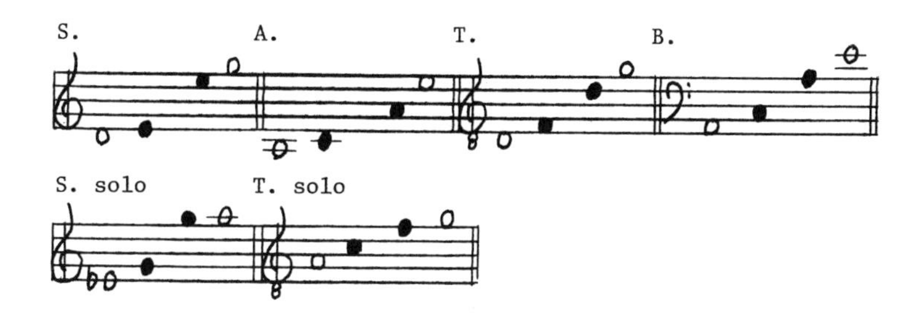


Avant-garde:

improvise on pitches supplied

Traditional:

Melody: little tonal feeling; very chromatic

Harmony: nonfunctional; chords built on seconds, fourths; frequent unisons; texture very thick

Rhythm: unmetered throughout; groupings of two, three, four eighth-note beats

## EYE CHART

Composer: Arthur Frackenpohl Author:

Publisher: Walton No. 2913 Price: $1.00

Voicing: SATB; S(A)T(B) solo[1] Grade: med Time: 4:10

Accompaniment: a cappella

Type of Text: vowels, consonants

Range and Tessitura: relative to singer

Avant-garde:

time segments (regular, irregular beats); graphic notation of pitch, rhythm, dynamics; specified seating of choir

Traditional: not applicable

[1]Solo short; of same nature as choral parts

## EYES OF ALL LOOK HOPEFULLY TO YOU, THE

Composer: Richard Felciano Author: biblical

Publisher: Apogee No. EMP-1854-3 Price:

Voicing: TTB (SSA) Grade: diff. Time:

Accompaniment: organ (use of pedals necessary)[1]

Type of Text: sacred; psalm 144; confidence in God

Range and Tessitura:

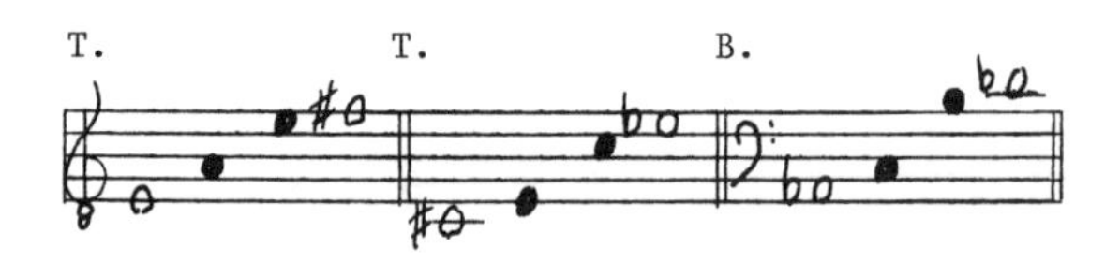


Avant-garde:

glissandos

Traditional:

Melody: little tonal feeling; very chromatic

Harmony: nonfunctional

Rhythm: changing meters (5/4, 4/4, 3/4, 3/8, 9/8, 12/8); syncopation; triplet eighths; combinations of eighths and sixteenths

---

[1]No reduction of voice parts; organ part usually contains pitch of voice parts in some manner

EZEKIEL (NINE PARABLES)[1]

Composer: Gerald Kemner    Author: biblical

Publisher: Walton    No. M-138    Price: $2.00

Voicing: SATB, div.    Grade: diff.    Time: 13:40

Accompaniment: electronic tape[2]

Type of Text: sacred/secular

Range and Tessitura:

Avant-garde:

ad libitum use of text; rhythmic speech; inflected rhythmic speech; spoken tone clusters; glissandos; whispering

Traditional:

Melody: tonal; chromatics; disjunct, conjunct

Harmony: functional; unison, two-part passages; sevenths; ninths; major/minor seconds between adjacent voices

Rhythm: changing meters within movements (4/4, 3/2, 2/4, 3/4, 5/4); triplet quarters, eighths; syncopation; combinations of eighths and sixteenths

---

[1]Nine movements; probably could be performed separately

[2]Tape - $10.00; two tracks: track A contains program heard by choir and audience, gives pitch cues; track B contains clicks which keep tempo of each movement - need separate amplifier and headset for conductor; piano score gives tape sound cues; no reduction of voice parts

FAITH COMETH BY HEARING

Composer: Carlton Young Author: biblical

Publisher: Hope No. CY 3343 Price: 40¢

Voicing: double choir; 3 soloists[1] Grade: easy Time:

Accompaniment: guitar; triangle; drums; tambourine; optional piano

Type of Text: sacred; true righteousness; salvation

Range and Tessitura:

Avant-garde:

graphic notation of pitch; rhythmic speech; glissando; ad libitum pitch, tempo, entrances; song-speech; improvisation

Traditional:

Melody: tonal; ostinato

Harmony: tonal; triadic

Rhythm: unmetered; triplet eighths

---

[1]Large and small choirs; each performs traditional and avant-garde music; choirs divided into men/women or high/low; soloists improvise a vocal line, use speech rhythm; speak text

FAMILY OF MAN, THE[1]

Composer: Michael Hennagin Author: Several[2]

Publisher: Walton No. M-117 Price: $2.50

Voicing: SATB[3] Grade: med. Time: 35:00

Accompaniment: 3 sets of brass wind-bells; educator bells; rhythm sticks; jangle clog; 4 small hand bells; alto recorder; suspended cymbal; large gong; 2 tom-toms; bongo drum; snare drum; vibraphone; chimes; orchestra bells; marimba; 3 timpani; tambourine; small gong; bass drum; flash lights; piano; electronic tape[4]

Type of Text: sacred/secular; celebration of man

Range and Tessitura:

Avant-garde:

inflected rhythmic speech; graphic notation of pitch; glissandos; ad libitum use of text; whispering; speaking; shouting; clapping; tongue clicks

Traditional:

Melody: tonal; conjunct; reciting on single pitch

Harmony: seconds between adjacent voices; parallel fourths, sixths; unison, two-part passages

Rhythm: changing meters (6/4, 4/4, 2/4, 3/4, 3/8, 7/8, 5/8, 5/4); free rhythm; syncopation; triplet quarters, eighths

---

[1]Work of six movements; can be performed separately; cf. Alike and Ever Alike, The Creation

[2]Carl Sandburg, James Joyce; Shakespeare, Homer, Kobadaishi

[3]Various voicings needed for different movements

[4]Tape available - $10.00; contains cues for entire work

[5]Low pitches sung in unison with another part

## FIRST CORINTHIANS 13

Composer: William McRae  Author: biblical

Publisher: Pepper  No. P010205  Price: 35¢

Voicing: SATB div.  Grade: med.  Time:

Accompaniment: a cappella (organ may give pitch if necessary)

Type of Text: sacred; Paul's description of "love"

Range and Tessitura:

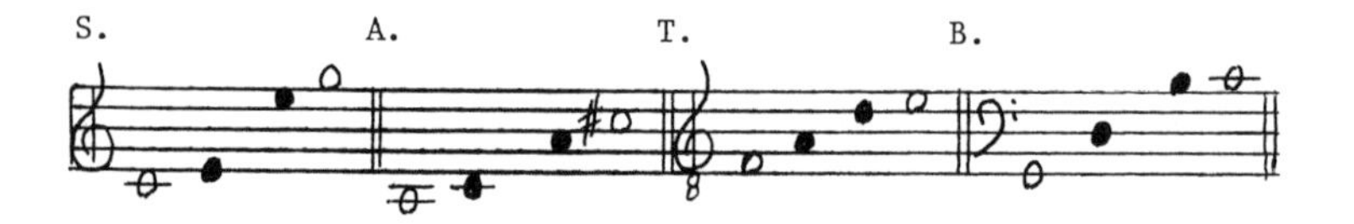


Avant-garde:

ad libitum pitch, rhythm; speaking; whispering; glissandos

Traditional:

Melody: tonal, modal; for most part conjunct; some chromatics

Harmony: nonfunctional; chords built in fourths; open fifths; major/minor seconds between adjacent voices; sevenths

Rhythm: unmetered

FIRST STAR

Composer: John Paynter Author: Anonymous

Publisher: Universal No. 15473 Price: 50¢

Voicing: unison[1] Grade: easy Time:

Accompaniment: metal percussion instruments (chime bars, glockenspiels, etc.) or piano

Type of Text: secular; nursery rhyme

Range and Tessitura:

All

Avant-garde:

ad libitum entrances, rhythms, tempo

Traditional:

Melody: tonal; chord patterns

[1]High voices preferable; final chord four-part

FOG

Composer: John Paynter Author: Elizabeth Paynter

Publisher: Universal No. 15477 Price: 65¢

Voicing: unison[1] Grade: med-easy Time:

Accompaniment: any suitable instruments

Type of Text: secular; mood evoking

Range and Tessitura:

Avant-garde:

ad libitum tempo, rhythm; individuals perform musical fragments ad libitum

Traditional:

Melody: tonal; disjunct

Harmony: aleatoric; final chord - minor seventh

Rhythm: ad libitum

---

[1]Changed or unchanged voices; one three-part chord at end

FRAGMENTS OF ARCHILOCHOS

Composer: Lukas Foss
Author: Archilochus[1]

Publisher: C. Fischer
No. 04652
Price: $10. 00

Voicing: 4 groups;[2] counter-tenor; male, female speakers
Grade: diff.
Time: 10:00

Accompaniment: mandolin, guitar;[3] percussion (three players)[4]

Type of Text: secular; fragments of ideas

Range and Tessitura:[5]

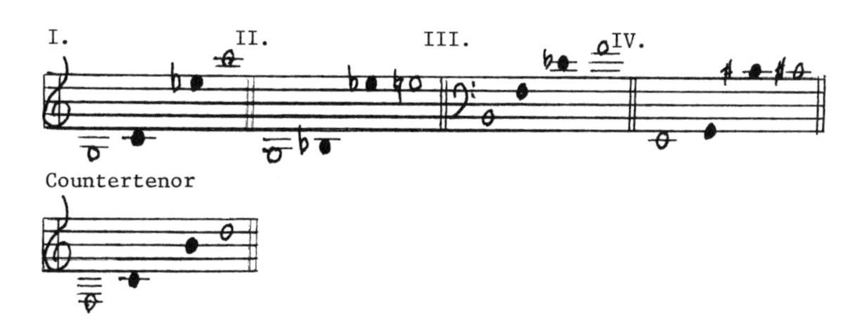


Avant-garde:

ad libitum use of musical phrases, performing forces, tempo, noises; tremulo; glissandos; murmuring; whispering; rhythmic speech; tone clusters; shouting

Traditional:

Melody: nontonal (pitch pipes recommended); disjunct, chromatic intervals

Harmony: nonfunctional; almost aleatoric

Rhythm: unmetered throughout, though 4/4 type notation used

---

[1]Translation from the Greek by Guy Davenport

[2]I: sopranos, mezzos; II: mezzos, altos; III: tenors, baritones; IV: baritones, basses; a large choir: I, II, III, IV - optional

[3]Mandolin, guitar notation partly proportional, indeterminate

[4]Small gongs; high, low gongs; drums; small, snare, bass; two pedal timpani; anvil or large pipe; woodblocks; temple blocks; chimes: chromatic, wooden, glass; antique cymbal; high, medium, low cymbals

[5]Note the voice combinations in each group (cf. #2 above) when considering the ranges

FREEDOM

Composer: Frederick Tillis Author:

Publisher: Southern No. SMP 2239-29 Price: $1.25

Voicing: SATB div. Grade: diff. Time:

Accompaniment: maracas, jingle bells

Type of Text: secular; civil rights protest

Range and Tessitura:

Avant-garde:

rhythmic speech; inflected rhythmic speech; whispering; glissandos

Traditional:

Melody: nontonal; chromatic; recitation on single pitch with tones added to form chords; cues for new pitches difficult

Harmony: nonfunctional; major/minor seconds, augmented fourths, diminished fifths between adjacent voices; many kinds of altered chords

Rhythm: changing meters (8/4, 4/4, 12/4, 6/4, 5/4, 3/4, 7/4); triplet quarters, eighths, sixteenths; combinations of eighths and sixteenths; polyrhythms

FUNERAL MARCH ON THE DEATH OF HEROES

Composer: Brock McElheran Author:

Publisher: Oxford No. 95.004 Price: 25¢

Voicing: unspecified Grade: easy Time:

Accompaniment: a cappella

Type of Text: secular; serious; funerial; names of the dead

Range and Tessitura: not applicable

Avant-garde:

ad libitum use of supplied, unsupplied text; tone clusters; spoken tone clusters; graphic notation of pitch

Traditional: not applicable

GARNETT

Composer: George Self Author:

Publisher: Universal No. 14320 Price: 35¢

Voicing: unison Grade: easy Time:

Accompaniment: drum; maraca; wood bars, xylophone; cymbal; glockenspiel, chime bars, metallophone; melodica, wind, or string instruments: these suggested, others may be substituted in the various categories

Type of Text: vowels, consonants; ad libitum text

Range and Tessitura: relative to individual singer

Avant-garde:

tone clusters; ad libitum tempo, rhythm, repetition of musical fragments; graphic notation of pitch, rhythm; tongue clicks; whistling; whispering

Traditional: not applicable

GEISTLICHE MUSIK or ADVENT-SURE ON OK CHORALES

Composer: Edwin London Author: hymn texts[1]

Publisher: Hope No. AG 7179 Price:

Voicing: 3 SATB choirs[2] Grade: diff. Time:

Accompaniment: orchestra: violins, violas, cellos, 2 trumpets, 2 trombones, 2 oboes, 2 bassoons; electronic tape;[3] optional - organ, tambourines, other percussion instruments to be played by choir #1

Type of Text: sacred; Advent, Lent

Range and Tessitura:

Avant-garde:

graphic notation of conductor's score ("Time is ordered by the horizontal dimension in the score") and dynamics; all music performed by choirs completely traditional in notation; instrumentalists improvise on supplied pitches, ad libitum performance of musical fragments

Traditional:

Melody: tonal; chromatic (voices and instruments)

Harmony: tonal; traditional hymn style modified by accidentals; augmented, diminished octaves, sevenths

Rhythm: traditional hymn style for voices; changing meters for brass (2/2, 3/2, 4/2, etc. up to 41/2); unmetered for woodwinds, strings

---

[1]Salvation Unto Us Has Come; Savior of the Nations, Come; Christ Jesus Lay in Death's Strong Bands

[2]One choir SATB soloists

[3]Tape available - $10.00

GENESIS

Composer: Elis Pehkonen  Author: biblical

Publisher: Universal  No. UE 15450  Price: $1.00

Voicing: three-part speaking chorus,[1] narrator  Grade: med-easy  Time: 5:30

Accompaniment: two electronic tapes;[2] keyboard instrument; suspended cymbal; sustaining instruments[3]

Type of Text: sacred; creation

Range and Tessitura: ad libitum; choice by singers

Avant-garde:

ad libitum entrance, use of supplied text; speaking and whispering of text; musical cells; graphic notation of pitch, rhythm, dynamics

Traditional:

Rhythm: traditional symbols used in music cells

---

[1]High, medium, low

[2]Electronic tape made by group; can get by with one tape recorder

[3]Instrumentalists sing as well as play; same music cells used as singers perform

GENESIS 21:6

Composer: Edwin London Author: biblical

Publisher: Agape No. AG 7170 Price: 90¢

Voicing: SATB[1] Grade: diff. Time: 6:20

Accompaniment: organ; 5 violins; viola; 2 cellos; bass (multiples of these if possible); flute; clarinet; bassoon; trumpet[2]

Type of Text: sacred/secular; "sacred" laughter

Range and Tessitura:

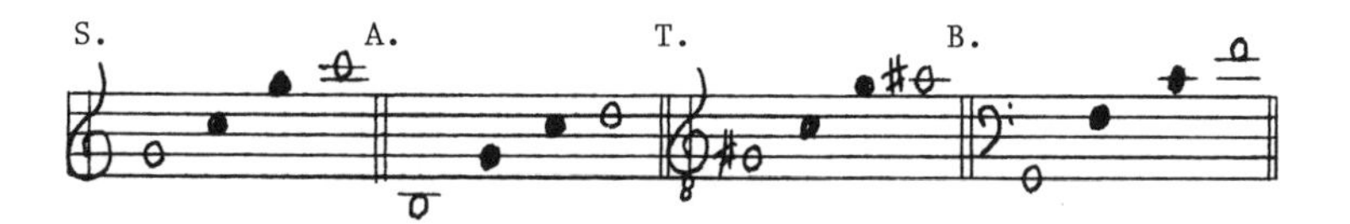

Avant-garde:

improvise laughter; glissandos

Traditional:

Melody: disjunct; long held pitches with laughter interspersed; little sense of "melody"; cues given by woodwinds

Harmony: nonfunctional; harmonies appear and dissolve with the laughter; organ and strings play a Bach choral one measure apart

Rhythm: choral parts unmetered; little rhythmic movement in the traditional sense

---

[1]Each section is in four parts; according to the composer, "to insure a steady state of textures with a convulsive edge." Each of the four parts sings the same pitch, but one or the other improvises laughter at various points.

[2]Strings play long sustained chords; winds must be able to improvise "chortles, copious chuckles, and stitch-splitting guffaws."

## GEOGRAPHICAL FUGUE

Composer: Ernst Toch Author:

Publisher: Belwin/Mills No. 60168 Price: 50¢

Voicing: SATB Grade: med-diff. Time: 2:00

Accompaniment: a cappella

Type of Text: secular; novelty

Range and Tessitura: not applicable

Avant-garde:

rhythmic speech

Traditional:

Rhythm: syncopation; three-against-two; combinations of eighths, sixteenths and thirty-seconds

GLORIA

Composer: Lars Edlund    Author:

Publisher: Hansen    No. WH 103    Price:

Voicing: SATB div; T. solo[1]    Grade: diff.    Time:

Accompaniment: a cappella[2]

Type of Text: sacred; Latin (Gloria from Latin mass)

Range and Tessitura:

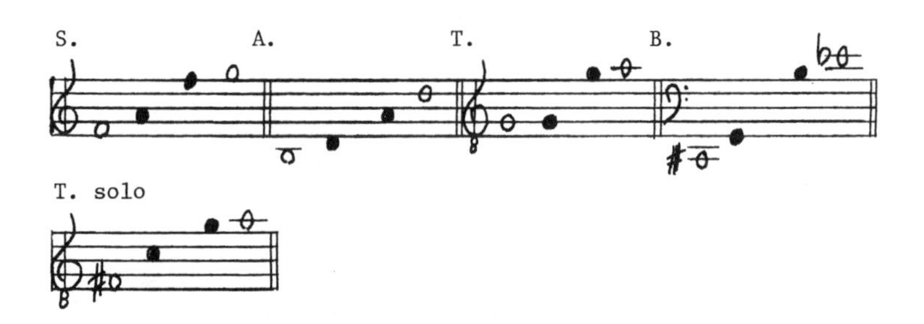


Avant-garde:

inflected rhythmic speech; quarter-tone; inflected rhythmic speech and singing combined; glissandos; written out tone clusters

Traditional:

Melody: nontonal; interval of minor seconds; microtones; chromatic; chant style

Harmony: nonfunctional, repetition gives some feeling of function; sevenths; major/minor seconds between adjacent voices

Rhythm: changing meters (4/4, 2/4, 3/8, 5/8, 3/4, 5/4, 3/2, 2/2, 6/4, 3/8); section where every measure or so is a change of meter; unmetered sections; combinations of eighths and sixteenths; triplet eighths, quarters; three-against-two; syncopation

---

[1]Solo part difficult; alto section performs spoken canon in five parts; sixteen voice chord builds as tone cluster - tone major/minor seconds apart

[2]No reduction of voice parts

GLORIA

Composer: Paul Patterson Author:

Publisher: Weinberger No. Price: $6.00

Voicing: SATB/SATB Grade: diff. Time:

Accompaniment: piano (two performers)[1]

Type of Text: sacred; Latin (Gloria in excelsis Deo)

Range and Tessitura:

Avant-garde:

graphic notation of pitch, rhythm; glissando; fragmentation of syllables; ad libitum pitch, use of text; shouting; inflected rhythmic speech; whispering; lip flapping; oscillating tone; open and closed mouth sounds

Traditional:

Melody: little melody in traditional sense; short fragments; whole and half steps; chromatic; voice crossings; much sliding from and to pitches

Harmony: nonfunctional; cluster sounds prominant; few chords in traditional sense

Rhythm: unmetered; traditional and nontraditional symbols used; time scale in seconds; the performance of music fragments

---

[1]No reduction of voice parts

[2]Top notes falsetto

GO TELL IT IN THE CITY

Composer: V. Earl Copes    Author: V. E. Copes

Publisher: Abingdon    No. APM-880 Price: 45¢

Voicing: SATB    Grade: med.    Time:

Accompaniment: organ (pedals necessary)

Type of Text: sacred; brotherhood

Range and Tessitura:

Avant-garde:

inflected rhythmic speech; ad libitum rhythmic speech

Traditional:

Melody: shifting tonality; chromatic; disjunct

Harmony: major/minor seconds, parallel fourths, fifths between adjacent voices; augmented, diminished chords; unisons, doublings at the octave

Rhythm: changing meters (4/4, 6/4, 9/8, 6/8, 5/4, 12/8); syncopation; triplet eighths, quarters; combinations of eighths and sixteenths

GOD IS

Composer: Carlton Young | Author: biblical
Publisher: Hope | No. CY 3339 Price: 30¢
Voicing: unison[1] | Grade: easy Time: 3:00[2]

Accompaniment: organ or piano; optional percussion (unspecified)

Type of Text: sacred; praise of God

Range and Tessitura:

Avant-garde:

rhythmic speech; glissando; clapping; improvisation if desired

Traditional:

Melody: tonal; unison; one melody repeated at intervals throughout the composition

Harmony: optional two-part choral part in parallel fourths

Rhythm: syncopation

[1]Congregation can be included

[2]Can be lenghtened or shortened as desired

GOD IS OUR REFUGE, GOD IS OUR STRENGTH

Composer: Hal H. Hopson | Author: biblical
Publisher: Warner | No. WB-181 Price: 40¢
Voicing: SATB[1] | Grade: med-easy Time:

Accompaniment: a cappella

Type of Text: sacred; Psalm 46; confidence in God

Range and Tessitura:

Avant-garde:

rhythmic speech; combination of rhythmic speech and singing

Traditional:

Melody: tonal; chordal outline; chanting on one pitch

Harmony: tonal; chords built in fourths; unison passages

Rhythm: changing meters (3/4, 2/4, 4/4); triplet eighths, quarters; three-against-two, three-against-four; combinations of eighths and sixteenths

---

[1]Occasional divisi of soprano and alto

GOD LOVE YOU NOW

Composer: Donald Erb Author: Thomas McGrath

Publisher: Merion No. 342-40099 Price: 50¢

Voicing: SATB div; soloists[1] Grade: diff. Time:

Accompaniment: 4 marine band harmonicas; 4 plastic slide-whistles; set of bongo drums; maracas; claves; castanets; tambourine; triangle; pop bottles; reverberation device[2]

Type of Text: sacred; anti-war

Range and Tessitura:

Avant-garde:

fragments of syllables; written-out tone clusters; glissandos; ad libitum rhythm; graphic notation of pitch; chest thumps

Traditional:

Melody: nontonal; chromatic; conjunct

Harmony: nonfunctional; augmented and diminished octaves; parallel minor thirds between adjacent voices; fifths, fourths of every type; clusters built from unison

Rhythm: unmetered sections; syncopation; triplet eighths, quarters; combinations of eighths and sixteenths

---

[1]Soloists drawn from sections; parts similar to what choir sings

[2]A tape recorder can be used as the reverberation device; directions supplied

GOSPEL ACCORDING TO JUDAS, THE

Composer: Ben Ludlow    Author: Ben Ludlow

Publisher: Flammer    No. A-5620    Price: 35¢

Voicing: SATB, narrator    Grade: med-easy    Time: 14:00

Accompaniment: organ; 2 cymbals; timpani (3 pitched drums: high, medium, low may be substituted)

Type of Text: sacred; a passion narrated by Judas

Range and Tessitura:

Avant-garde:

glissando; written tone cluster; whispering; moaning

Traditional:

Melody: tonal; disjunct; some chromatics

Harmony: tonal; built in fourths; built up by adding voices

Rhythm: changing meters (7/4, 4/4); long sustained chords, little rhythmic movement

[1]Narrator important; he carries the main weight of the composition; choir acts as "Greek chorus"

GOTTA BE SPRING

Composer: Ben Ludlow Author:

Publisher: Shawnee No. A-1214 Price: 30¢

Voicing: two-part Grade: easy Time: 1:00

Accompaniment: suspended cymbal; castanets; tambourine

Type of Text: secular; celebrates spring

Range and Tessitura: not applicable

Avant-garde:

rhythmic speech

Traditional:

Rhythm: syncopation

GROWING UP FREE

Composer: Bert Konowitz
Author:
Publisher: Alfred
No. 6711
Price: 60¢
Voicing: two-part[1]
Grade: med-easy
Time:

Accompaniment: piano; guitar, bass, drums - optional

Type of Text: secular; freedom for all; scat syllables

Range and Tessitura:

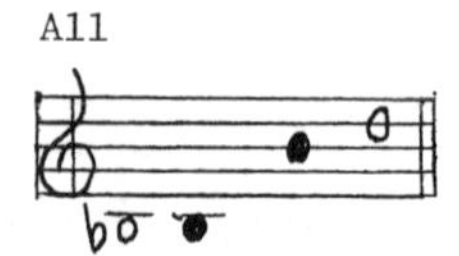


Avant-garde:

rhythmic speech; finger snaps; vocal improvisations (suggestions concerning rhythm, pitches offered); dance movements improvised (suggestions offered)

Traditional:

Melody: tonal; shifting tonality; chromatics; ostinatos

Harmony: functional; ostinatos; major seconds between adjacent voices

Rhythm: syncopation

[1]Can be performed as unison

HAND AND FOOT, THE

Composer: Jay Paul Krush
Author: Jones Very
Publisher: C. Fischer
No. CM 7955
Price: 50¢
Voicing: SATB
Grade: diff.
Time:

Accompaniment: organ;[1] trumpet; trombone; two sets of tubular chimes

Type of Text: sacred; creation under God's law

Range and Tessitura:

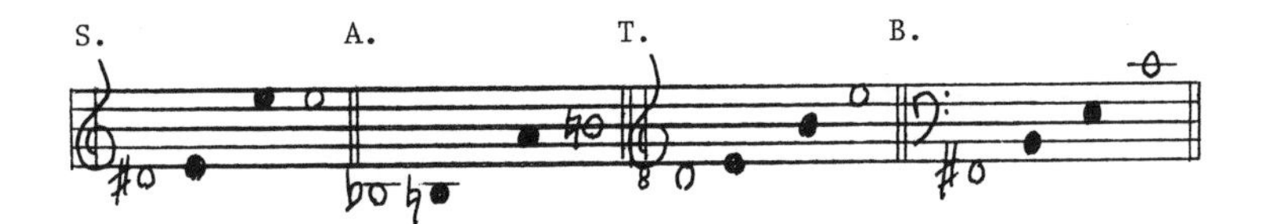


Avant-garde:

ad libitum pitch (highest, lowest notes individuals can sing: tone cluster effect is desired)

Traditional:

Melody: nontonal; disjunct; chromatic; fourths prominant

Harmony: nonfunctional; two intervals of a fourth superimposed a second apart; augmented, diminished chords of every type

Rhythm: changing meters (4/4, 3/4, 2/4, 7/8, 5/4); triplet quarters; polyrhythms between voices and accompaniment

---

[1]Pedals necessary; organ part independent of voice parts

HAVE YOU HEARD?

Composer: Ben Ludlow  Author: Ben Ludlow

Publisher: Shawnee  No. A-1215  Price: 30¢

Voicing: three-part  Grade: easy  Time: 1:12

Accompaniment: finger cymbals; snare drum; bass drum

Type of Text: sacred; Christmas

Range and Tessitura: not applicable

Avant-garde:

rhythmic speech; whispering

Traditional:

Rhythm: syncopation; triplet quarters

HE KEEPS ME SINGING

Composer: David Knowles
Author: Luther R. Bridges
Publisher: Crescendo
No. CP-343
Price: 40¢
Voicing: two-part (SB)
Grade: easy
Time:
Accompaniment: piano
Type of Text: sacred; praise of Jesus
Range and Tessitura:

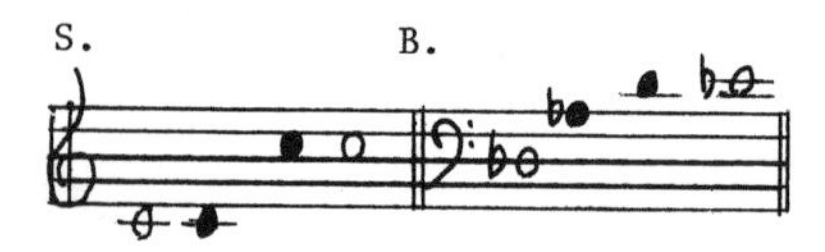


Avant-garde:

rhythmic speech

Traditional:

Melody: tonal; conjunct

Harmony: functional; parallel thirds

Rhythm: syncopation

HE THAT HATH EARS

Composer: Carl Zytowski
Author:[1]
Publisher: World Library
No. CA-7528-8
Price:
Voicing: SATB div.; SAT soloists
Grade: diff.
Time:
Accompaniment: vibraharp; timpani; five unpitched drums[2]

Type of Text: secular; seeking peace

Range and Tessitura:

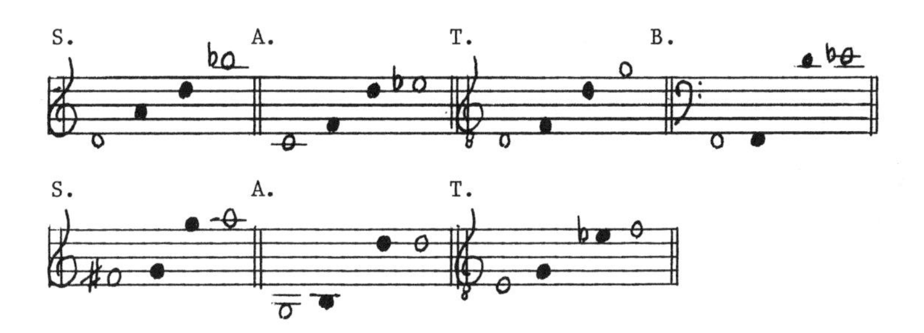


Avant-garde:

inflected rhythmic speech; rhythmic speech; ad libitum rhythm; tone clusters; glissandos; graphic notation of pitch; repetitions of vowels, consonants

Traditional:

Melody: nontonal; chromatics; conjunct, disjunct; (major/minor seconds, fifths)

Harmony: nonfunctional; two-part passages; major/minor seconds between adjacent voices; altered chords of various types; aleatoric

Rhythm: unmetered throughout; traditional symbols used; much unison rhythmic movement

---

[1]The Revelation of St. John the Divine, John F. Kennedy, Martin Luther King, Robert F. Kennedy

[2]Instrumental parts available (IN-7529); no reduction of voice parts

HERE COMES THE AVANT-GARDE

Composer: Brock McElheran Author:

Publisher: Oxford No. 95.005 Price: 60¢

Voicing: open[1] Grade: med. Time: 15:00[2]

Accompaniment: piano; following optional: timpani, chimes, bongos, snare drum, güiro, claves; vibraphone, xylophone, marimba, cymbals; electronic tape - optional[3]

Type of Text: secular, novelty

Range and Tessitura: relative to individual singer

Avant-garde:

fragments of every type of avant-garde idiom and sound

Traditional:

three fragments of tonal, traditionally notated music

[1]Ten singer minimum; any arrangement

[2]Parts can be left out ad libitum

[3]Choir must prepare the tape if it is to be used

HIGH SCHOOL BAND, THE

Composer: John Paynter Author: Reed Whittemore

Publisher: Oxford No. 84.238 Price: 65¢

Voicing: SSATB div.; S. solo Grade: diff. Time: 4:00

Accompaniment: a cappella

Type of Text: secular; novelty

Range and Tessitura:

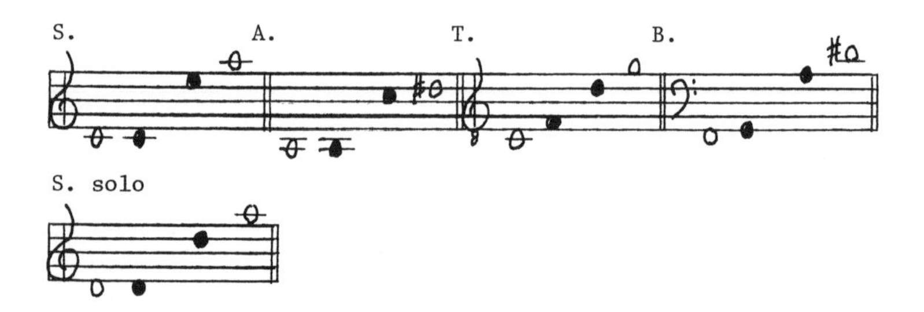

Avant-garde:

ad libitum rhythm tempo, entrances

Traditional:

Melody: tonal, chromatic; disjunct; augmented, diminished intervals

Harmony: nonfunctional; chords built in fourths; augmented, diminished chords of all types; augmented and diminished intervals of every type between adjacent voices

Rhythm: changing meters (9/8, 2/4, 3/4, 12/8); triplet eighths; two-against-three, three-against-four; syncopation

HIST WHIST

Composer: R. W. Jones Author: e. e. cummings

Publisher: Shawnee No. a-1076 Price: 30¢

Voicing: SATB Grade: easy Time: 1:00

Accompaniment: optional percussion (suggested: snare drum, triangle, bass drum, suspended cymbal)

Type of Text: secular; novelty; Halloween

Range and Tessitura: relative to individual singers

Avant-garde:

inflected rhythmic speech; glissando; voice qualities to match words (ghostly, squeaky, etc.); whispering

Traditional:

Rhythm: syncopation

HOGAMUS, HIGAMUS

Composer: Arthur Frackenpohl Author: Anonymous

Publisher: Piedmont No. 4347 Price: 35¢

Voicing: three-part Grade: med. Time: 2:45

Accompaniment: percussion (three groups: metal, wood, membranes: each to have low, medium, high instruments)

Type of Text: secular; novelty

Range and Tessitura: relative to individual singer

Avant-garde:

rhythmic speaking; glissandos; graphic notation of pitch (high, medium, low)

Traditional:

Rhythm: changing meters (6/8, 9/8, 3/4); section of 6/8 meter against 2/4 meter; syncopation

HOMMAGE A HEINRICH SCHÜTZ

Composer: Milko Kelemen Author: biblical

Publisher: Peters No. 5977 Price:

Voicing: SATBB div.[1] Grade: diff. Time:

Accompaniment: a cappella[2]

Type of Text: sacred; Latin (no English translation supplied); Psalm 120: 1-4; call to God for deliverance

Range and Tessitura:

Avant-garde:

rhythmic speech; improvised rhythmic speech; singing and rhythmic speech combined; glissandos; whispering; laughing; repetition of consonants; shouting; written-out tone clusters

Traditional:

Melody: nontonal; chromatic; conjunct, disjunct

Harmony: nonfunctional; major/minor seconds between adjacent voices; writing is very polyphonic with harmony resulting from the flow of the lines

Rhythm: changing meters (4/4, 3/8, 6/8, 5/4, 3/4, 6/4); each line has own rhythm; triplet eighths; five sixteenths and more to beat; three-against-two; three-against-four

---

[1]Solo lines appear for each part which are to be sung by section members

[2]No reduction of voice parts

N. B. tempo, expressive terms are in German

HONEYWELL

Composer: Howard Rees Author:

Publisher: Universal No. UE 15453 Price: 65¢

Voicing: three-part Grade: easy Time:

Accompaniment: three groups of instruments may be used; no specifications

Type of Text: none supplied

Range and Tessitura: relative to individual singers

Avant-garde:

ad libitum pitch, assignment of musical fragments; fragments of melody, rhythm, chords interpreted by each group

Traditional:

Melody: tonal

Harmony: triads; sevenths; optional

Rhythm: elementary 3/4 meter

HOW EXCELLENT IS THY NAME

Composer: Eugene Butler | Author: biblical
Publisher: Bourne | No. | Price: 60¢
Voicing: SSA[1] | Grade: easy | Time:
Accompaniment: piano or organ
Type of Text: sacred; Psalm 8 adaptation
Range and Tessitura:

Avant-garde:

rhythmic speech and singing combined

Traditional:

Melody: tonal; scale, chord patterns

Harmony: functional; unisons; sevenths

Rhythm: triplet quarters, eighths; combinations of eighths and sixteenths; unison rhythmic movement

[1]Available in SATB, SAB arrangements

HUMANA SINE NOMINE

Composer: William Penn | Author: biblical, composer
Publisher: Heritage | No. H 105 | Price: 90¢
Voicing: TTBB;[1] speaker | Grade: med-easy | Time:
Accompaniment: piano;[2] suspended cymbal; hand drum
Type of Text: sacred; Luke 2:29-32; uselessness of death through war

Range and Tessitura:[3]

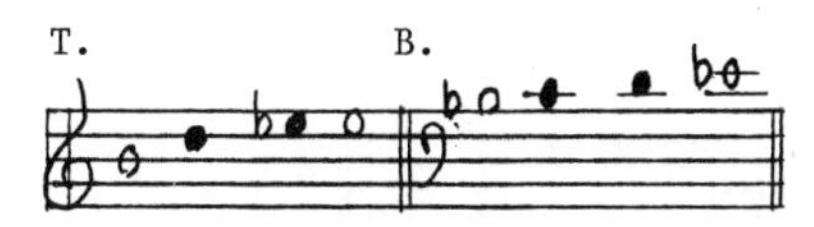


Avant-garde:

rhythmic speech; ad libitum tempo, conductor's cues; whispering; choreography; hand claps; finger snaps

Traditional:[4]

Melody: nontonal; conjunct; each part has its own melodic pattern to repeat ad libitum

Harmony: one chord (two minor seconds a diminished octave apart); remainder aleatoric

Rhythm: changing meters (3/4, 4/4, 2/4, 12/8, 3/8); combinations of eighths and sixteenths

---

[1]Can be performed SATB or SSAA; directions given for substitutions; speaker performs rhythmic speech

[2]Need grand piano; pianist must read accidentals

[3]Make octave adjustments for other voicings

[4]Approximately six measures of traditionally notated music

HYMN OF THE UNIVERSE

Composer: Richard Felciano Author: Teilhard de Chardin

Publisher: E. C. Schirmer No. 2944 Price:

Voicing: SAB Grade: med. Time: 3:50

Accompaniment: electronic tape[1]

Type of Text: sacred; God, source/support of universe

Range and Tessitura:

Avant-garde:

ad libitum rhythm; glissando; musical fragments (cells) performed according to a time scale in seconds (need stop watch); sing with electronic tape accompaniment

Traditional:

Melody: isolated notes, figures; chromatic; diminished intervals between fragments

Harmony: overlapping and performance of several fragments together result in harmony; nonfunctional; dissonant; aleatoric

Rhythm: polymeters; some fragments metered, others unmetered

[1]Tape supplies cues for entrances, pitches

I MUST SHOUT HIS PRAISE

Composer: Bob Burroughs Author: Leslie Brandt

Publisher: Beacon Hill No. AN-6016 Price: 30¢

Voicing: SATB[1] Grade: med-easy Time:

Accompaniment: organ or piano

Type of Text: sacred; praise of God

Range and Tessitura:

Avant-garde:

speaking (solo and choir)

Traditional:

Melody: tonal; some chromatics; disjunct

Harmony: functional; chords with added notes; major/minor seconds, fourths between adjacent voices

Rhythm: syncopation; unison rhythm prominent

I SAW AN ANGEL

Composer: Daniel Pinkham Author: biblical

Publisher: E. C. Schirmer No. 2973 Price:

Voicing: SATB; SATB soloists Grade: med Time: 4:00

Accompaniment: electronic tape

Type of Text: sacred; praise; alleluia

Range and Tessitura:

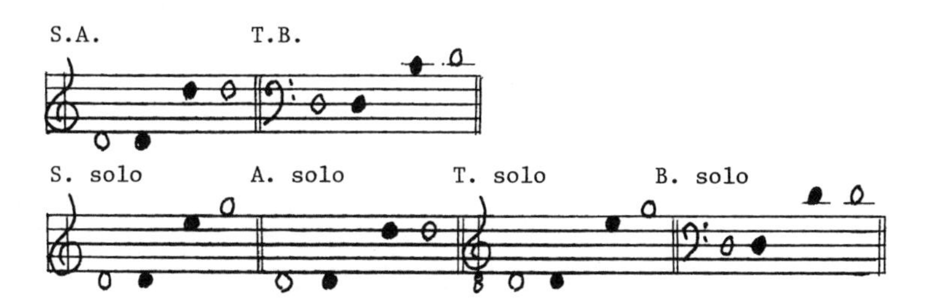


Avant-garde:

melodic fragments; ad libitum rhythm, tempo, entrances; time segments

Traditional:

Melody: varying patterns of descending D minor scale

Harmony: aleatoric

Rhythm: (soloists only: triplet eighths in unmetered segments); rhythms for choir totally ad libitum

## I WAS A GULL ONCE

Composer: Sydney Hodkinson Author: Keith Gunderson

Publisher: Merion No. 342-40104 Price: 40¢

Voicing: SA div;[1] SA soloists Grade: med-diff. Time: 1:50

Accompaniment: a cappella[2]

Type of Text: secular; novelty

Range and Tessitura:

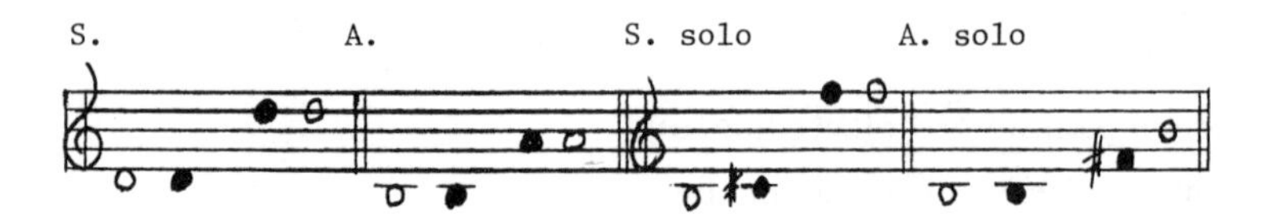


Avant-garde:

improvisation on supplied pitches; ad libitum performance of text

Traditional:

Melody: chromatic; shifting tonal centers; fourths, fifths, major/minor seconds prominent

Harmony: nonfunctional; major/minor seconds between adjacent voices; dissonance created by improvisation on pitches which are half-step apart

Rhythm: syncopation; triplet eighths, quarters; complex between two solo voices

---

[1]Alto divided into five parts

[2]No reduction of voice parts

IDENTITY

Composer: David Mathew Author:
Publisher: Oxford No. 95.312 Price: 60¢
Voicing: unspecified[1] Grade: easy Time: 3:30
Accompaniment: a cappella
Type of Text: secular; serious
Range and Tessitura: not applicable

Avant-garde:

rhythmic speech; ad libitum entrances; choreography

Traditional:

Rhythm: syncopation; unison rhythmic movement

[1]Sixteen performers or multiples of sixteen needed

IF YOU RECEIVE MY WORDS

Composer: Knut Nystedt Author: biblical
Publisher: Augsburg No. 11-9214 Price: 60¢
Voicing: SATB div. Grade: diff. Time: 6:00
Accompaniment: a cappella[1]
Type of Text: sacred; Proverbs 2:1-15, 3:1-4
Range and Tessitura:

Avant-garde:

unmetered sections; speaking

Traditional:

Melody: tonal; fourths, fifths; augmented, diminished intervals; chromatic

Harmony: nonfunctional; open parallel fifths; major/minor seconds between adjacent voices; sevenths, ninths, elevenths, augmented, diminished chords; unison passages

Rhythm: changing meters (2/2, 3/2, 4/2, 5/2, 6/2, 7/4, 4/4, 3/8, 3/4, 7/8); syncopation

---

[1]No reduction of voice parts

[2]Low notes in unison with Alto

IN JUST

Composer: James Yannatos  Author: e. e. cummings

Publisher: Associated  No. A-648  Price: 30¢

Voicing: SSATB[1]  Grade: diff.  Time:

Accompaniment: a cappella

Type of Text: secular; spring

Range and Tessitura:

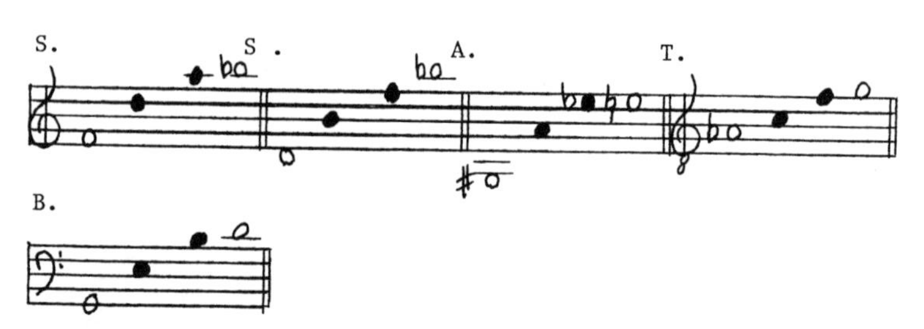


Avant-garde:

inflected rhythmic speech; glissando; fragments of syllables; whistling; whispering; audible inhaling

Traditional:

Melody: nontonal; disjunct; augmented, diminished intervals

Harmony: nonfunctional; chords with added tones

Rhythm: changing meters (3/4, 2/4, 1/4, 4/4); combinations of eighths and sixteenths; triplet eighths, sixteenths; syncopation; three-against-two

---

[1]Occasional tenor, bass divisi

## IN THE BEGINNING OF CREATION

Composer: Daniel Pinkham    Author: biblical

Publisher: Ione    No. 2902    Price:

Voicing: SATB[1]    Grade: easy    Time: 3:00

Accompaniment: electronic tape

Type of Text: sacred; Genesis 1:1-3

Range and Tessitura:

Avant-garde:

glissando; tone clusters; whispering; inflected rhythmic speech; graphic notation of pitch; ad libitum rhythm; improvise melody to text; sing with electronic tape sounds

Traditional:

Melody: nontonal; fragments; minor second, augmented sevenths, diminished ninths

Harmony: one chord: C major with added second and augmented fourth

Rhythm: unmetered sections; triplet eighths

[1]Unison except for final chord which is divisi

IN THE PRESENCE

Composer: Gilbert Trythall Author: G. T. Seaborg
Publisher: Marks No. 4495 Price: 65¢
Voicing: SATB[1] Grade: diff. Time: 5:25
Accompaniment: electronic tape[2]
Type of Text: secular; novelty; atomic age terminology
Range and Tessitura:

Avant-garde:

rhythmic speech; tone clusters; glissandos; fragmentation of syllables; whispering

Traditional:

Melody: tonal, shifting tonality; chromatic; conjunct; cross voices

Harmony: occasionally nonfunctional; major/minor seconds between adjacent voices

Rhythm: three-against-two; syncopation; triplet eighths, sixteenths

[1]Occasional soprano, alto divisi chord

[2]Tape - $8.00

INCARNATIO

Composer: R. Sherlaw Johnson Author: biblical

Publisher: Oxford No. X 227 Price: 60¢

Voicing: SSATB[1] Grade: diff. Time:

Accompaniment: a cappella[2]

Type of Text: sacred; Latin; birth of Christ

Range and Tessitura:

Avant-garde:

fragments of syllables; prolongation of consonant sounds

Traditional:

Melody: nontonal; isolated pitches; disjunct

Harmony: nonfunctional; altered chords of every type; sevenths, ninths appear but do not function in traditional manner

Rhythm: changing meters (4/4, 3/2); syncopation, but movement is slow; isolated single pitch entries; triplet quarters, eighths; polyrhythms

---

[1]Bass divisi on long sustained chords

[2]No reduction of voice parts

INVENTION FOR VOICES AND TAPE

Composer: John Biggs Author:

Publisher: Gentry No. g-166 Price: 50¢

Voicing: SATB[1] Grade: easy Time:

Accompaniment: electronic tape[2]

Type of Text: secular; awareness of "on the brink"

Range and Tessitura:

Avant-garde:

ad libitum pitch, entrances; whispering; shouting; speaking; clapping; improvise melody in imitation of tape; choreography

Traditional:

Melody: descending scale

Harmony: aleatoric

Rhythm: changing meters (6/4, 3/4, 2/4, 7/4, 5/4)

---

[1]Tape - $5.95

[2]Any combination of four differently pitched voices possible; four soloists perform a unison passage

KYRIE

Composer: Donald Erb  Author:

Publisher: Merion  No. 342-40026  Price: 45¢

Voicing: SATB div.  Grade: diff.  Time:

Accompaniment: electronic tape; 4 suspended cymbals; 4 woodblocks; temple blocks; 2 snare drums; bass drum (with foot pedal); 1 timpani; xylophone; vibraphone; set of large claves; set of small claves; bongos; maracas

Type of Text: sacred; from Catholic mass; Greek: Kyrie eleison

Range and Tessitura:

Avant-garde:

fragmentation of words; glissandos; relative pitch; finger snaps; kissing sound; tongue clicks; hiss; ad libitum pitch, rhythm, various sounds suggested; graphic notation of pitch; whispering; shouting; modification of sounds with hands

Traditional:

Melody: singing on one or two pitches, almost a chant; nontonal; much sliding from pitch to pitch

Harmony: written out tone clusters; only an occasional chord in traditional sense; sevenths

Rhythm: complex; unmetered sections; combinations of eighths and sixteenths; triplet eighths, quarters; two-against-three; syncopation

KYRIE

Composer: Paul Patterson Author:

Publisher: Weinberger No. Price: $2.50

Voicing: SATB div. Grade: diff. Time:

Accompaniment: piano; two players, one manipulates the strings inside

Type of Text: sacred; from Catholic mass; Greek: Kyrie eleison; syllables

Range and Tessitura:

Avant-garde:

relative pitch, graphic notation of pitch, tempo, rhythm; time segments in seconds but "these are only approximate lengths"; musical fragments; glissandos; modify sound with hands; clapping; shouting; fragmentation of syllables; half-speaking; ad libitum tempo

Traditional:

Melody: singing on one or two pitches, almost chanting; some intervals of octave, fourths, thirds; no tonal feeling composition as a whole though a fragment may have a tonal feeling; unison pitches indicated

Harmony: little in traditional sense for choir; much dissonance because of freedom of execution by sections or individuals

Rhythm: unmetered time segments; mostly written as quarters, eighths; only an occasional "ensemble" passage

## LAMENT FOR A LOST CHILD

Composer: Jere Hutcheson  Author:

Publisher: Walton  No. 2921  Price: 40¢

Voicing: SATB, S. soloist[1]  Grade: med.  Time: 4:00

Accompaniment: a cappella[2]

Type of Text: vowels, syllables to create mood

Range and Tessitura:

Avant-garde:

ad libitum change of tone quality (pinch nose, pat hand on mouth); glissandos; tone clusters; ad libitum slides, glissandos; claps; foot stomps; approximate notation of pitch

Traditional:

Melody: long sustained notes; disjunct ostinato on chord; chromatic ostinato

Harmony: nonfunctional; parallel thirds between adjacent voices; contrary motion of thirds between men and women voices

Rhythm: changing meters (4/4, 3/4, 8/4, 7/4, 6/4, 1/4); only one section with definite metric feeling

---

[1]Solo may be performed by boy soprano or woman

[2]No reduction of voice parts

LAMENT OF DAVID, THE

Composer: Daniel Pinkham Author: biblical

Publisher: E. C. Schirmer No. 2939 Price: 50¢

Voicing: SATB, div. Grade: diff. Time:

Accompaniment: electronic tape

Type of Text: sacred; 2 Samuel 1:19-29; mourning death of Saul

Range and Tessitura:

Avant-garde:

ad libitum pitch, use of text; murmuring; humming

Traditional:

Melody: nontonal; chromatic; disjunct; augmented, diminished intervals of every type

Harmony: nonfunctional; seconds, sevenths, augmented, diminished octaves between adjacent voices; unison, two-part passages

Rhythm: changing meters (4/4, 3/8, 2/4, 12/8, 9/8, 6/8, 3/4, 5/8); cross rhythms; syncopation; triplet eighths; combinations of eighths and sixteenths

LAMENT OF JOB, THE

Composer: Dale Jergenson Author: biblical

Publisher: G. Schirmer No. 12030 Price: 75¢

Voicing: SATB div, soloists[1] Grade: med-diff. Time:

Accompaniment: a cappella

Type of Text: sacred; varying sentiments from book of Job

Range and Tessitura:

Avant-garde:

tone clusters; ad libitum pitch, rhythm, glissandos; graphic notation of pitch, rhythm; free improvisation; improvisation on rhythms supplied; cluster melodies; mumbling; rhythmic whispering; humming; combined whispering and singing

Traditional:

Melody: tonal, modal, chromatics; shifting tonalities; conjunct

Harmony: functional; occasional nonfunctional; chords built on fourths; seconds between adjacent voices; sevenths, ninths; triads a second apart superimposed

Rhythm: changing meters (4/4, 3/4, 6/4, 5/4); unmetered sections; triplet eighths, quarters; syncopation

[1]Sixteen solo voices, any combination, needed to chant on ad libitum pitches, staggered entrances

LANDSCAPES (A CHORAL SUITE)

Composer: John Paynter    Author: T. S. Eliot

Publisher: Oxford    No. 337785 3    Price:

Voicing: SATB div.    Grade: diff.    Time: 12:30

Accompaniment: a cappella; optional oboe interludes[1]

Type of Text: secular; descriptive, mood creating; serious

Range and Tessitura:

Avant-garde:

ad libitum performance of musical fragments (melodies and rhythms supplied); ad libitum tempo, rhythm, entrances

Traditional:

Melody: great variety; tonal; nontonal; chromatic; disjunct

Harmony: nonfunctional, some functional; altered chords, sevenths, ninths, elevenths

Rhythm: changing meters (6/8, 12/8, 9/8, 2/4, 4/4,

3/8); each movement has a variety of meters; syncopation; combination of free rhythm and metered rhythms and musical fragments; combinations of eighths and sixteenths; triplet eighths, sixteenths; duplets in triple meters

---

[1]No reduction of voice parts

[2]B-II on pedal point for all of 2nd movement, high F in unison with tenors

LAST WORD, THE

Composer: Bert Konowitz Author:

Publisher: Alfred No. Price: 40¢

Voicing: SATB div. Grade: med. Time:

Accompaniment: piano[1]

Type of Text: secular, scat syllables; happiness is ...

Range and Tessitura:

Avant-garde:

improvisation; ad libitum speaking, singing, chanting of text

Traditional:

Melody: tonal, disjunct, chromatic

Harmony: jazz chords, sevenths, ninths; major seconds between adjacent voices

Rhythm: syncopation; triplet eighths

---

[1]Must be able to read accidentals; no reduction of voice parts

LET THE FLOODS CLAP THEIR HANDS

Composer: Ben Ludlow    Author: biblical
Publisher: Flammer    No. A-5673    Price: 30¢
Voicing: three-part choir[1]    Grade: easy    Time: 1:05
Accompaniment: cymbals; snare drum; bass drum
Type of Text: sacred; psalm 98; praising
Range and Tessitura: not applicable

Avant-garde:

rhythmic speaking; clapping

Traditional:

Rhythm: syncopation

[1]Suggested three contrasting voice qualities be used

LET THE REDEEMED OF THE LORD SAY SO

Composer: Eugene Butler    Author: biblical
Publisher: Hinshaw    No. HMC-168    Price: 45¢
Voicing: SATB div.    Grade: med.    Time:
Accompaniment: keyboard[1]
Type of Text: sacred; confidence in God
Range and Tessitura:

Avant-garde:

rhythmic speech; rhythmic speech and singing combined

Traditional:

Melody: tonal; some chromatics; conjunct, disjunct

Harmony: functional; altered chords

Rhythm: changing meters (4/4, 2/4, 3/4); combinations of eighths and sixteenths; syncopation

[1]Some facility needed

LET THE SPIRIT SOAR

Composer: Brock McElheran Author: Brock McElheran

Publisher: Oxford No. 94.006 Price: 40¢

Voicing: any[1] Grade: easy Time:

Accompaniment: electronic tape optional[2]

Type of Text: sacred

Range and Tessitura:

All

Avant-garde:

ad libitum rhythm, tempo; whispering

Traditional:

Melody: pentatonic

Harmony: occurs by chance (pentatonic)

[1]Congregation or audience can be involved

[2]Tape available from publisher; organ can substitute

LIFE A QUESTION

Composer: Eugene Butler Author: Corrine R. Robinson
Publisher: C. Fischer No. CM 7801 Price: 30¢
Voicing: SATB div. Grade: med. Time: 1:30
Accompaniment: a cappella
Type of Text: secular; serious; humanistic
Range and Tessitura:

Avant-garde:

rhythmic speech; ad libitum tempo, whispering

Traditional:

Melody: tonal; chromatic; conjunct; chord patterns

Harmony: functional sevenths, ninths, added tones; widely spaced chords built on triads a second apart

Rhythm: changing meters (2/2, 6/8); syncopation; triplet quarters

MAD MADRIGALS

Composer: Jerry F. Davidson Author: Shakespeare
Publisher: Walton No. 2922 Price: 40¢
Voicing: SATB;[1] SATB soloists Grade: med. Time:
Accompaniment: a cappella
Type of Text: secular; from the Sonnets of Shakespeare; variety of moods from somewhat serious to very serious
Range and Tessitura: relative to individual singers

Avant-garde:

ad libitum pitch; graphic notation of pitch; shouting

Traditional:

Melody: modal fragments; most melody simply suggested through graphic notation

Harmony: nonfunctional; aleatoric

Rhythm: changing meters (6/8, 2/4, 4/4); unmetered; triplet eighths

---

[1]Entire choir divided into four small groups, more or less equal in number and sex. At times one soloist selected from each group to determine pitch for group or entire choir.

MAGNIFICAT

Composer: Alec Wyton

Author: biblical

Publisher: Agape

No. AG 7127 Price: 35¢

Voicing: SATB, A. soloist[1]

Grade: med-diff.

Time:

Accompaniment: a cappella

Type of Text: sacred; praise of God for helping the lowly

Range and Tessitura:

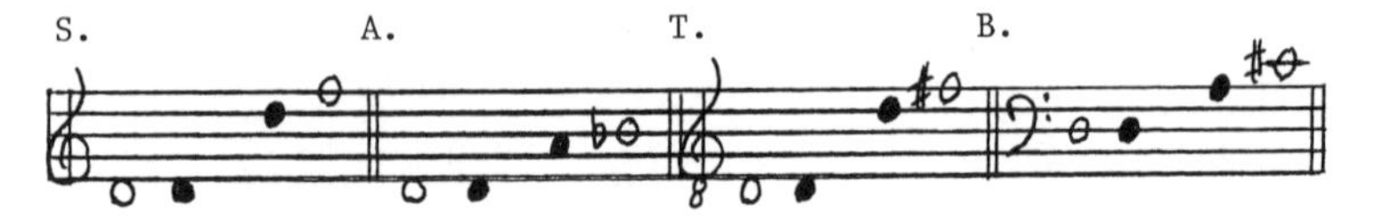


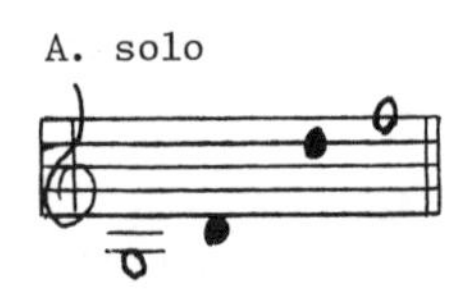

Avant-garde:

ad libitum rhythm, tempo

Traditional:

Melody: nontonal; chanting on single pitch; octaves, fifths, fourths

Harmony: nonfunctional; chords built in fourths, fifths; diminished octaves between adjacent voices

Rhythm: unmetered throughout; traditional rhythmic notation used; triplet quarters, eighths; combinations of eighths and sixteenths

---

[1]Solo long, difficult; melody disjunct, nontonal; rhythm is complex though marked "very free"; solo part only rarely moves rhythmically against the choral parts

MASS WITH ELECTRONIC TAPE

Composer: Gregory Woolf  Author:

Publisher: World Library  No. CA 2006-8  Price:

Voicing: SATB, div.[1]  Grade: med-diff.  Time:

Accompaniment: organ, electronic tape[2]

Type of Text: sacred; English mass text (no creed)

Range and Tessitura:

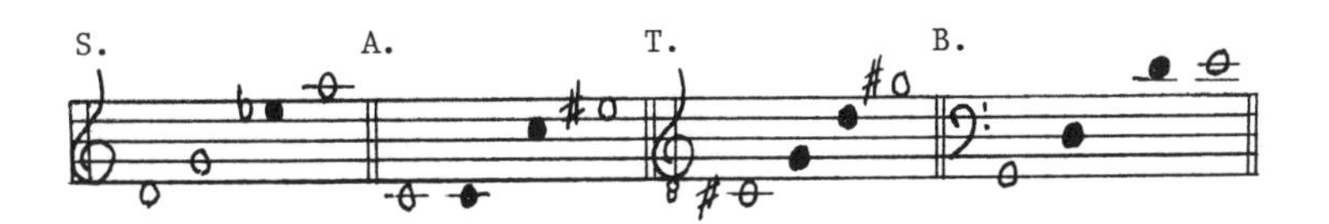


Avant-garde:

all choral parts traditionally notated; tone clusters achieved by a building of chords by additions at half-step intervals

Traditional:

Melody: tonal, modal; polymodal; cross voices; chromatics; melodic patterns repeated

Harmony: functional; major/minor seconds between adjacent voices; chords build in seconds; patterns repeated; unison passages

Rhythm: changing meters between and within movements; within movements (4/4, 3/4; 4/4, 3/4, 6/4; 3/4, 4/4, 3/8, 5/4, 6/8); much unison rhythmic movement; unmetered sections; free rhythm

[1] Soprano has from 1 to 4 parts; alto has from 1 to 5 parts; tenor has from 1 to 4 parts; bass has from 1 to 5 parts

[2] No reduction of voice parts; organ supports the vocal lines

MAY MAGNIFICAT[1]

Composer: John Paynter  Author: Gerard Manley Hopkins

Publisher: Oxford  No. 343692 2 Price:

Voicing: SATB[2]  Grade: diff.  Time: 6:30

Accompaniment: a cappella[3]

Type of Text: secular/sacred; beauty of creation

Range and Tessitura:

Avant-garde:

ad libitum performance of musical cells (fragments), entrances, rhythms, tempo; pitches supplied, rhythms improvised

Traditional:

Melody: tonal, nontonal; chromatic; conjunct, disjunct

Harmony: nonfunctional; built in fourths; parallel fourths in adjacent voices; major/minor seconds between adjacent voices; unisons

Rhythm: changing meters (4/4, 2/4, 3/8, 5/8, 3/4, 3/2); section where one choir in 4/4, another in 3/4, others unmetered; triplet quarters, eighths; combinations of eighths and sixteenths

[1]Three choruses; may be performed separately

[2]Some divisi in S. B. in first composition; SSAA voicing for second; two choirs: SA and SSATB in third composition

[3]No reduction of voice parts

MEDUSA - THE SHIP

Composer: Ronald Sindelar Author: Ronald Sindelar

Publisher: Walton No. 2912 Price: $1.00

Voicing: SATB div. 2 SAT soloists[1] Grade: diff Time:

Accompaniment: electronic tape; claves; wood block; suspended cymbal; tam-tam; snare, field, tenor, bass drums; four chromatic tympani; (five percussionists required, some must improvise)[2]

Type of Text: secular; shipwreck

Range and Tessitura:

Avant-garde:

ad libitum repetitions, entrances, tempo; improvisation on pitches supplied; tone clusters written out; laughing; whispering; humming; graphic notation of pitch; audible inhale/exhale; glissandos

Traditional:

Melody: nontonal; chromatics; disjunct; diminished octaves

Harmony: nonfunctional; major/minor seconds between adjacent voices; aleatoric

Rhythm: unmetered (time expressed in seconds); 4/4 passages with half, quarter, eighth, notes

---

[1]Basses subdivided into four for tone clusters; difficult soloists' parts

[2]Percussion parts available - $1.00

MESSA D'OGGI[1]

Composer: Eskil Hemberg    Author: Salvatore Quasimodo, Dag Hammarskjold

Publisher: Hansen    No. WH 104    Price:

Voicing: SATB;[2] SSATB soloists    Grade: diff.    Time:

Accompaniment: a cappella[3]

Type of Text: sacred; Greek (Kyrie); Latin (Gloria) Italian, English, confidence in God, mass texts

Range and Tessitura:

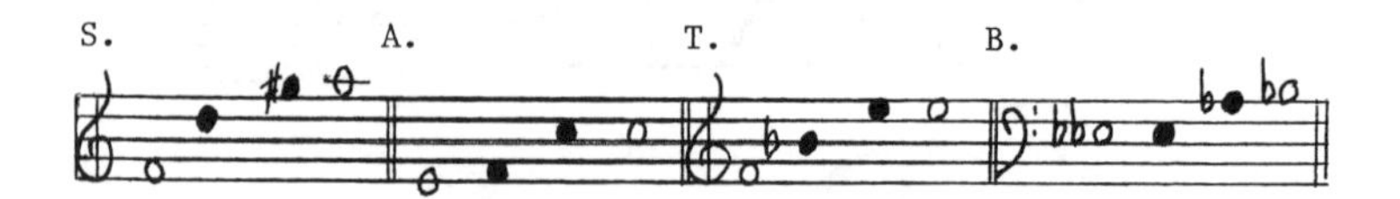

Solos:

Avant-garde:

fragmentation of words; syllables distributed; graphic notation of pitch, rhythm; tone clusters; whispering; sighing; shouting; ad libitum rhythm; glissandos

Traditional:[4]

Melody: nontonal; isolated pitches; modal chants; conjunct

Harmony: nonfunctional; major/minor seconds between adjacent voices; modal harmonies for chant melodies

Rhythm: choir always unmetered; soloists: syncopation; triplets

---

[1]Three compositions, five movements; could be performed separately

[2]SATB divisi into four each to form clusters; perform rhythmic chant

[3]No reduction of voice parts

[4]Soloists traditional notation; choir chants on pitch, form clusters in fifth movement; other movements either soloists alone or choir alone

MINI-MOTET FROM MICAH

Composer: Thomas Beversdorf   Author: biblical

Publisher: Southern   No. SC-24   Price: 50¢

Voicing: SATB; Bar., Coloratura solos   Grade: diff.   Time:

Accompaniment: organ or harpsichord, bass

Type of Text: sacred; prophetic utterances against "sinners"

Range and Tessitura:

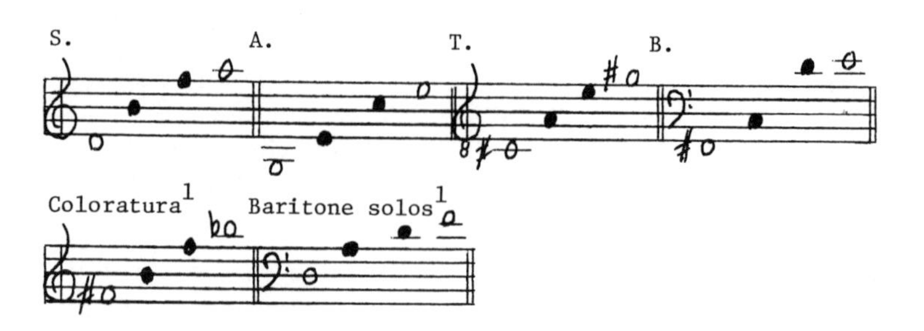


Avant-garde:

ad libitum use of text, rhythm

Traditional:

Melody: nontonal; disjunct; chromatic

Harmony: nonfunctional, nontonal; major/minor seconds between adjacent voices; altered chords; added tones

Rhythm: changing meters (4/4, 5/4, 3/4); syncopation; crossed rhythms; triplet quarters

---

[1]Solos are difficult; more complex melodically and rhythmically than choral parts

MINIMUSIC

Composer: R. Murray Schafer Author:

Publisher: Universal No. 15449 Price: $1.00

Voicing: unspecified[1] Grade: med-easy Time:

Accompaniment: a cappella[2]

Type of Text: ad libitum

Range and Tessitura: not applicable

Avant-garde:

ad libitum pitch, rhythm; graphic notation of pitch, rhythm; free improvisation; improvisation on pitches supplied

Traditional: traditional embellishment symbols, dynamic, and rhythmic symbols used

---

[1]Any number of singers, but small enough that the performers can listen to each other

[2]Composition may be performed by a group of instruments or a group of singers. No directions concerning combining groups, though the possibility seems to exist.

MINIWANKA (THE MOMENTS OF WATER)

Composer: R. Murray Schafer Author:

Publisher: Universal No. 15573 Price: $2.95

Voicing: SA or SATB;[1] S. solo Grade: med. Time: 4-5:00

Accompaniment: a cappella

Type of Text: secular; American Indian words for water

Range and Tessitura:

Avant-garde:

ad libitum pitch, entrances; graphic notation of pitch, rhythm, dynamics; glissandos; trilled "R"; tone clusters; rhythmic speech; whispering

Traditional:

Melody: tonal; conjunct

Harmony: unisons; triads; aleatoric

Rhythm: changing meters (4/4, 2/4, 6/8, 3/8)

---

[1]Seven various solo voices needed to perform canon section

[2]Only pitches specified for T. B.

## MOODY'S LOBSTERS

Composer: Sydney Hodkinson  Author: Keith Gunderson
Publisher: Merion  No. 342-40102  Price: 30¢
Voicing: TB  Grade: easy  Time: :45
Accompaniment: a cappella
Type of Text: secular; novelty
Range and Tessitura: not applicable

Avant-garde:

half-spoken, half-sung style (inflected rhythmic speech); glissandos

Traditional:

Rhythm: changing meters (2/4, 3/4); triplet quarters; three-against-four; syncopation; combinations of eighths and sixteenths

## MOON CANTICLE[1]

Composer: Leslie Bassett  Author:
Publisher: Peters  No. 66270  Price:
Voicing: SATB div.; S, A soloists,[2] male, female narrators  Grade: diff.  Time: 17:00
Accompaniment: cello obligato[3]
Type of Text: secular; aspects of moon and its mythology

Range and Tessitura:

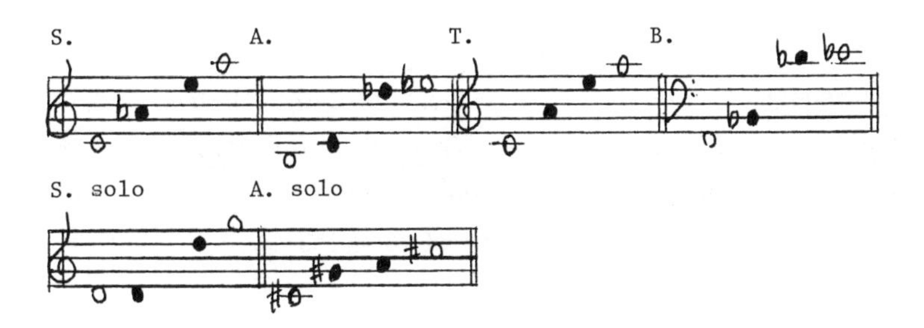


Avant-garde:

inflected rhythmic speech; prolongation and repetition of consonants; cluster glissandos; rhythmic speech and singing combined; tone clusters improvised speech; ad libitum entrances, tempo

Traditional:

Melody: nontonal; chromatics; conjunct, disjunct

Harmony: nonfunctional; doublings at the octave; major/minor seconds between adjacent voices; chords built in fourths

Rhythm: changing meters (2/4, 3/4, 2/2, 3/2; 7/8, 3/4, 2/4, 5/8; 3/4, 2/4, 4/4, 5/4; 6/8, 3/8, 9/8; 4/4, 2/4); frequent meter changes; unmetered sections; duplets in 6/8 meter; triplet quarters, eighths, sixteenths; syncopation; combinations of eighths, sixteenths and thirty-seconds

---

[1]Consists of five movements; could perform separately

[2]Composer remarks that soloists need absolute pitch, though pitch pipes could be used to aid in hearing cue pitches

[3]No reduction of voice parts

MUSCLES AND THE BONES THAT CARRY US TO LOVE, THE[1]

Composer: Gerald Kemner  Author: Dan Jaffe

Publisher: Walton  No. M-140  Price: $2.00

Voicing: SATB div.  Grade: diff.  Time: 11:15[2]

Accompaniment: electronic tape[3]

Type of Text: secular; variety of thoughts

Range and Tessitura:

Avant-garde:

ad libitum shouting of text; glissandos; rhythmic speech; graphic notation of rhythm

Traditional:

Melody: variety for different movements; tonal, nontonal; chromatic; conjunct, disjunct

Harmony: variety: functional, nonfunctional; repetition of progressions gives functional feeling; sevenths prominent; parallel fourths; unison, two-part passages; major/minor seconds between adjacent voices

Rhythm: changing meters (4/4, 2/4, 3/4, 5/4; 4/4, 6/4); triplet eighths, quarters; syncopation

---

[1]Work consists of eight movements; some could be performed separately or in smaller groups

[2]Total time; movements: 1:30, 0:30, 2:30, 1:45, 1:30, 0:30, 1:15, 1:45

[3]Tape supplies pitch cues; piano score provided for rehearsal; no reduction of voice parts

MUSIC FOR THE ASCENSION

Composer: Elliott Schwartz Author: Elliott Schwartz

Publisher: C. Fischer No. CM 7773 Price: 35¢

Voicing: SATB, narrator Grade: diff. Time: 6:30

Accompaniment: organ;[1] suspended cymbal; 3 tenor drums or tom-toms

Type of Text: sacred; petition; praise of God, Christ

Range and Tessitura:

Avant-garde:

glissandos; improvise on supplied pitches; ad libitum tempos, entrances; whispering

Traditional:

Melody: tonal, very chromatic; much recitation on pitch; entering pitch difficult to "hear" at times; accompaniment does not support the melodies

Harmony: functional, but very chromatic; chords with added tones; altered tones

Rhythm: complex; triplet eighths with many ties; five-sixteenths to beat; three-against-two; syncopation; combination of eighths and sixteenths

---

[1]Organist must be skilled, especially in rhythm; play clusters, glissandos; part independent from the voice parts

MY CATS

Composer: Elis Pehkonen Author: Stevie Smith

Publisher: Universal No. 15422 Price: 65¢

Voicing: 3-pt choir; narrator Grade: easy Time:

Accompaniment: 2 glockenspiel; 4 drums; xylophone; piano; small gong; suspended cymbal; triangle; tambourine; maraca

Type of Text: secular; novelty

Range and Tessitura: not applicable

Avant-garde:

ad libitum use of text; time segments; graphic notation of pitch, rhythm

Traditional:

Rhythm: traditional symbols occasionally used but without any exact meaning

NAUTICAL PRELUDES[1]

Composer: Lars Johan Werle Author:

Publisher: Hansen No. WH 108 Price: $2.50

Voicing: SATB div.;[2] SATB soloists[3] Grade: diff. Time:

Accompaniment: a cappella[4]

Type of Text: secular; about ships and the sea

Range and Tessitura: solo parts lie within the ranges

Avant-garde:

written-out tone clusters; rhythmic speech; improvisation on text; whispering; glissandos; rhythmic speech and singing combined; fragmentation of words; natural speaking of text

Traditional:

Melody: nontonal; chromatic; isolated pitchs; cues difficult to hear; cross voices

Harmony: nonfunctional; repetition of progressions give feeling of function; major/minor seconds between adjacent voices; close voicing - cluster effect frequent; octave doublings in large chords; augmented, diminished octave in same chord

Rhythm: changing meters (9/8, 6/8, 4/4, 12/8) syncopation; triplet eighths; four in time of three, five in time of four; combinations of eighths and sixteenths

---

[1]Six movements performed "attacca"

[2]Divisi can call for eight-part chord in a section; three-, four-voice chords in a section not uncommon

[3]At least eight singer-soloists per section; composer indicates how many are to sing each solo line; three-, four-part chords not unusual; movements three, four, five call for soli choir versus full choir

[4]No reduction of voice parts

NEW IS OLD, THE

Composer: Lloyd Pfautsch    Author: biblical

Publisher: Abingdon    No. APM-855    Price: 40¢

Voicing: SATB; unison;[1] soloist[2]    Grade: med-easy    Time:

Accompaniment: guitar; bass; drums; (organ may substitute)

Type of Text: sacred; praising

Range and Tessitura:

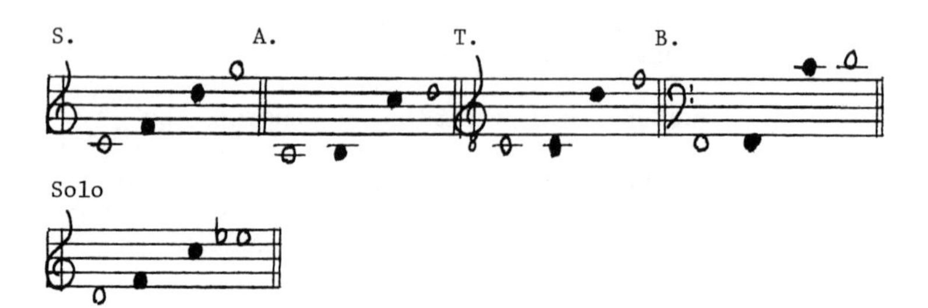


Avant-garde:

rhythmic speech

Traditional:

Melody: tonal; conjunct; change of key

Harmony: tonal; functional ostinato accompanying figures; much unison, two part singing

Rhythm: changing meters (3/4, 4/4, 5/4); syncopation; combinations of eighths and sixteenths

---

[1]For congregation or unison choir

[2]Unspecified

NIGHT SPEECH

Composer: Nicolas Roussakis Author:

Publisher: Continuo No. Price:

Voicing: four-part choir Grade: med-diff Time: 8:00

Accompaniment: pails of water; sandpaper; wind chimes of varying pitch and quality (brass, bamboo, shell, etc.); high and low gongs; two instrumentalists needed; harmonicas for each singer

Type of Text: secular; novelty; mood evoking; vowels, consonants[1]

Range and Tessitura: not applicable

Avant-garde:

rhythmic speech; voiced and unvoiced (whispering) sounds

Traditional:

Rhythm: polyrhythms abound (two-against-three, three-against-four, five-against-six); triplet eighths; syncopation

---

[1]International phonetic alphabet used; table supplied

90TH PSALM, THE[1]

Composer: Paul Seiko Chihara Author: biblical

Publisher: Shawnee No. A 1098 Price: $2.00

Voicing: SATB div.[2] Grade: diff. Time: 25:00

Accompaniment: organ;[3] brass quintet (two trumpets, two trombones) - optional

Type of Text: sacred; Psalm 90 (every verse expressed at least in part)

Range and Tessitura:

Avant-garde:

rhythmic speech; rhythmic speech and singing combined; glissandos; ad libitum rhythm

Traditional:

Melody:[4] nontonal; chromatics

Harmony:[4] nonfunctional; major/minor seconds between adjacent voices

Rhythm: changing meters (between movements and within movements): (within: 2/4, 3/8; 3/8, 4/8; 4/4, 3/4, 6/4; 4/4, 5/4, 3/4; 2/2, 3/4); polyrhythms; free rhythm against traditionally notated rhythms; triplet quarter, half notes; syncopation; duplet quarters in 3/8 meter

---

[1]17 movements of varying lengths (one for each verse of the psalm); suggestions given for performance of selected movements

[2]Score calls for various combinations with SATB divisi in three subsections, each in one movement

[3]No reduction of voice parts (open score of 12 staffs in one movement)

[4]Music derived largely from a three-chord progression and a 12-tone row

NOTA

Composer: Jan Bark    Author:

Publisher: Hansen    No. 11898    Price: 50¢

Voicing: SSATBB[1]    Grade: med.    Time: 10:00

Accompaniment: a cappella (source for pitch may be used)[2]

Type of Text: vowels, consonants

Range and Tessitura:

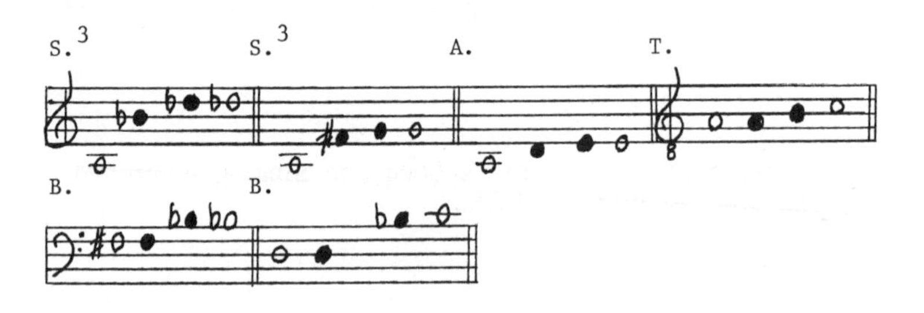

Avant-garde:

glissandos; graphic notation of pitch; trills; ad libitum endings; choreography (very important to the musical effect); ad libitum rhythm, tempo, pitch

Traditional:

Melody: ostinato patterns (half-step alternation); low sustained pitches; glissandos used with all pitch changes

Harmony: nonfunctional; major/minor seconds between adjacent voices; harmonic changes created by one or more voices moving by half-step; an ostinato type of harmonic movement

Rhythm: many tied notes over the bar, but the slow tempo dispells any feelings of syncopation

---

[1]"Solo" voices in each section give the pitch; twenty-three singers recommended as the size of the group

[2]No reduction of voice parts

[3]Low notes in unison with Alto part

NOT-YET FLOWER, THE

Composer: Richard Felciano Author: biblical

Publisher: E. C. Schirmer No. 2937 Price: 35¢

Voicing: unison[1] Grade: easy Time: 1:45[2]

Accompaniment: electronic tape; some kind of bell

Type of Text: sacred; beginning of Gospel of John

Range and Tessitura:

Avant-garde:

ad libitum text (news items); electronic accompaniment: lighting

Traditional:

Melody: modal

Harmony: singing is against a drone octave from the tape

Rhythm: unmetered (traditional rhythmic symbols used); syncopation

[1]Second part can be created if desired

[2]Sung portion is only part of an "event"

O BEAUTIFUL! MY COUNTRY![1]

Composer: Daniel Pinkham    Author: Philip Freneau, Anne Bradstreet, James Russell Lowell

Publisher: Ione    No. 3021    Price

Voicing: SATB div.    Grade: diff.    Time:

Accompaniment: piano - optional[2]

Type of Text: secular; patriotic; revolutionary

Range and Tessitura:

Avant-garde:

glissandos; tone clusters[3]

Traditional:

Melody: nontonal; chromatic; disjunct; leaps of octave or more

Harmony: nonfunctional; occasional feeling of function; chords containing augmented, diminished octaves; altered chords of every type; major/minor seconds between adjacent voices

Rhythm: changing meters (4/4, 3/4; 2/4, 4/4, 3/4); triplet eighths; syncopation; three-against-two; much unison rhythmic movement

---

[1]Three movements; can be performed separately

[2]Piano part a reduction of voice parts with octave doublings

[3]Appear only in 1st movement; others totally traditional in notation

O DEPTH OF WEALTH

Composer: Daniel Pinkham Author: biblical

Publisher: E. C. Schirmer No. 2951 Price:

Voicing: SATB div. Grade: diff. Time:

Accompaniment: organ and electronic tape

Type of Text: sacred; Romans 11:33-36; praise

Range and Tessitura:

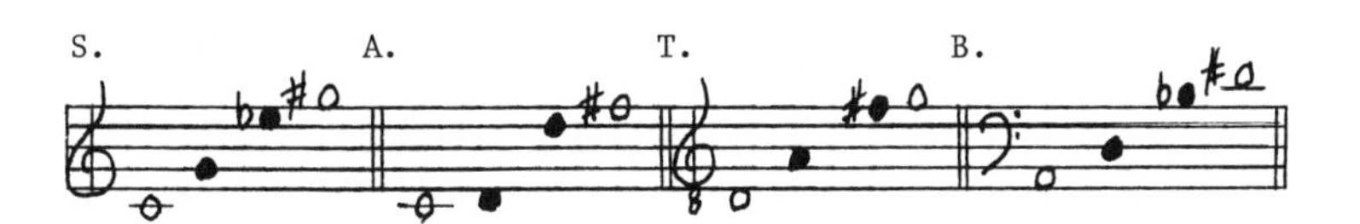


Avant-garde:

everything the choir performs is traditionally notated; choir performs at one point with electronic tape background

Traditional:

Melody: usually tonal; shifting tone centers; chromatic; disjunct at times; nontonal in one section

Harmony: nonfunctional many times; major/minor seconds between adjacent voices; augmented, diminished octaves; chromatically altered chords; unison and two part passages; organ supports harmonies

Rhythm: changing meters (4/4, 2/4); syncopation; choir and organ move in rhythmic unison

OUT OF SIGHT

Composer: Richard Felciano Author:

Publisher: E. C. Schirmer No. 2909 Price: 45¢

Voicing: SATB Grade: med. Time: 4:00

Accompaniment: electronic tape; organ

Type of Text: sacred/secular; ascension joined with ecology

Range and Tessitura:

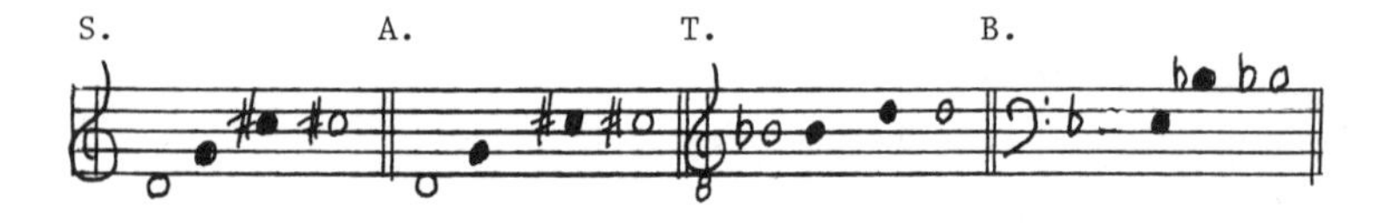


Avant-garde:

rhythmic speech; rhythmic speech and singing combined; ad libitum use of text

Traditional:

Melody: chanting on one pitch; interval of seventh occurs repeatedly; minor seconds frequent

Harmony: minor seconds between adjacent voices; sevenths; unisons between two parts

Rhythm: changing meters (2/4, 4/4, 5/4, 3/4, 6/4); triplet eighths; triplet against eighths or sixteenths; syncopation

OZYMANDIAS

Composer: Willard A. Palmer  Author: Percy B. Shelley

Publisher: Alfred  No.  Price: 30¢

Voicing: SATB, male soloist  Grade: easy  Time:

Accompaniment: a cappella

Type of Text: secular; Shelley poem

Range and Tessitura: relative to individual singer

Avant-garde:

ad libitum pitch; entire piece an "improvisation"; ad libitum rhythm; graphic notation of pitch

Traditional:

Rhythm: changing meters (3/4, 4/4)

---

[1]Soloist must be able to improvise a dramatic melody; one singer from each section selects a pitch which entire section then adopts

PATH OF THE JUST, THE

Composer: Knut Nystedt  Author: biblical

Publisher: Augsburg  No. 11-9333  Price: 55¢

Voicing: SATB div. [1]  Grade: diff.  Time:

Accompaniment: a cappella[2]

Type of Text: sacred; Proverbs 4:18-23; the just man praised, admonished

Range and Tessitura:

Avant-garde:

tone cluster effect

Traditional:

Melody: tonal; shifting tonalities; chromatics; ostinato and imitative passages

Harmony: nonfunctional but ostinato repetitions give some feeling of function; major/minor seconds between adjacent voices; triads moving in parallel motion

Rhythm: changing meters (4/2, 3/2, 2/2); unmetered sections with eighth note pulse; two-against-three-against-four; triplet quarters; much unison rhythmic movement

---

[1]Soprano, alto each four-part divisi for round, tenor three-part divisi for same purpose; SA have written out three-part passage

[2]No reduction of voice parts

PATRIOT'S DREAM, THE

Composer: Buryl Red Author: Katherine LeeBayes

Publisher: General No. Price:

Voicing: SATB div. Grade: med. Time:

Accompaniment:

Type of Text: patriotic

Range and Tessitura:

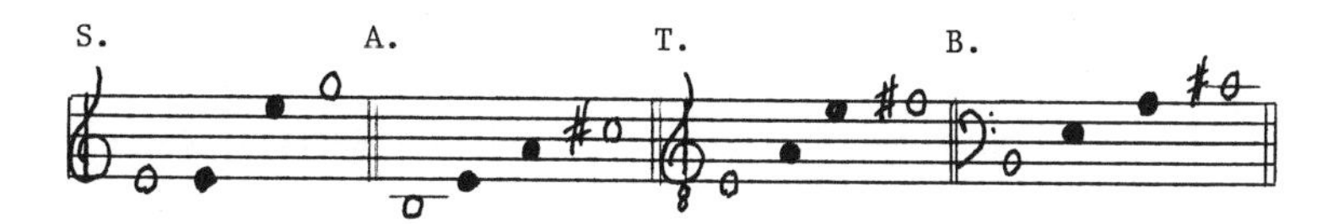


Avant-garde:

inflected rhythmic speech

Traditional:

Melody: tonal; some chromatics; scale, chordal patterns

Harmony: functional; unison, two-part passages; sevenths, chords built in fourths; parallel thirds over ostinatos

Rhythm: triplet eighths, sixteenths; combinations of eighths and sixteenths

PENTECOST SUNDAY - DOUBLE ALLELUIA

Composer: Richard Felciano Author: biblical; Roman mass

Publisher: World Library No. EMP-1532-1 Price: 35¢

Voicing: unison (male) Grade: med-easy Time: 3:00

Accompaniment: organ;[1] electronic tape

Type of Text: sacred; alleluia; coming of Holy Spirit

Range and Tessitura:

Avant-garde:

ad libitum entrances, use of text; glissandos; whispering; modification of sound with hands

Traditional:

Melody: nontonal; chromatic; sliding between pitches

Rhythm: changing meters (4/4, 6/4, 2/4, 5/4); triplet eighths; syncopation; unmetered sections (stop watch needed)

---

[1]Organist must be able to read accidentals

PETITIONS FOR HELP

Composer: Richard P. Hoffman Author: St. Patrick

Publisher: Augsburg No. 11-3000 Price: 10¢

Voicing: SATB div. [1] Grade: easy Time: 2:34

Accompaniment: organ

Type of Text: sacred; general anthem

Range and Tessitura:

Avant-garde:

speaking; speaking with singing; rhythmic speech; ad libitum pitch, tempo; musical fragments[1]

Traditional:

Melody: tonal; scale fragments

Harmony: web of sound created by varying entrances

Rhythm: traditional notation throughout; eighths, quarters

---

[1]Soprano and alto sing same fragment; tenors and basses sing same fragment; varying entrances performed as an SATB div. choir

PITY THIS BUSY MONSTER, MANUNKIND

Composer: Ron Caviani Author: e. e. cummings

Publisher: Foster No. MF 321 Price: 45¢[1]

Voicing: SATB div.; narrator Grade: diff. Time:

Accompaniment: electronic tape[2]

Type of Text: secular; "philosophical"; about the world condition

Range and Tessitura:

Avant-garde:

glissandos; fragmentation of words; speaking; improvisation of melody to text and rhythms supplied; ad libitum pitch, rhythm; graphic notation of pitch

Traditional:

Melody: nontonal; very chromatic; disjunct; tonal section with shifting tonal centers

Harmony: nonfunctional; some unisons; major/minor seconds, altered fourths, fifths, augmented, diminished intervals of many types between adjacent voices

Rhythm: unmetered sections; sections where traditional symbols used (no meter given but 2/4 effect present); syncopation

---

[1]Tape - $7.50

[2]No reduction of voice parts

[3]Composer states: "Chords can be fairly loose since the effect is one of going nowhere."

[4]Low notes performed with alto

PLOT AGAINST THE GIANT, THE

Composer: Peter Westergaard Author: Wallace Stevens

Publisher: Boonin No. B. 142 Price: 50¢

Voicing: SSA; SSA soloists[1] Grade: diff. Time: 4:00

Accompaniment: clarinet; cello; harp (piano may substitute)[2]

Type of Text: secular; sinister, plotting

Range and Tessitura:

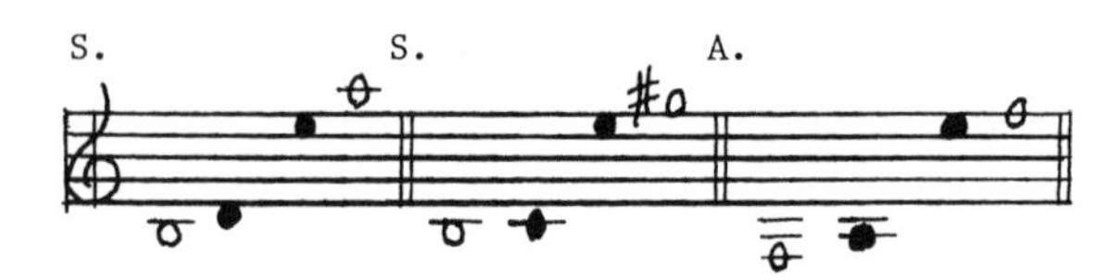


Avant-garde:

glissandos; portamentos; unspecified pitch

Traditional:

Melody: nontonal; very disjunct; chromatic; many augmented, diminished intervals

Harmony: nonfunctional; augmented, diminished intervals between adjacent voices; unison passages

Rhythm: changing meters (3/4, 2/4); syncopation; combinations of eighths and sixteenths; triplet eighths

POLONIUS PLATITUDES, THE[1]

Composer: Edwin London Author: Shakespeare

Publisher: Boonin No. B 132 Price: 60¢

Voicing: TTBB, div. Grade: diff. Time:

Accompaniment: a cappella

Type of Text: secular; novelty

Range and Tessitura:[2]

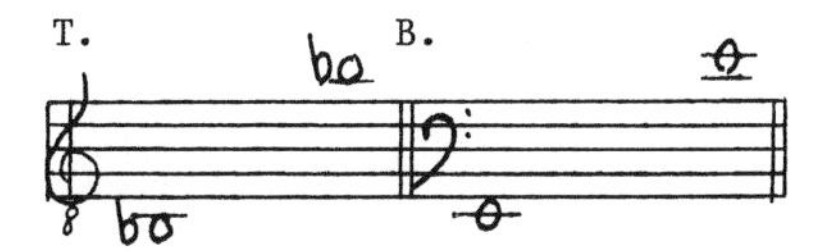


Avant-garde:

ad libitum performance of musical fragments, rhythms, dynamics; rhythmic speech; graphic notation of dynamics; tone clusters written out; use of balloons for visual and sonic effects

Traditional:[3]

Melody: variety throughout the composition; tonal, non-tonal; chromatics; conjunct, disjunct

Harmony: variety throughout the composition; functional, non-functional; aleatoric

Rhythm: changing meters between and within movements (within: 4/4, 6/8, 9/8; 3/2, 3/4; 3/8, 2/8, 4/4, 3/2); unmetered

---

[1]Seven movements; apparently can be performed separately

[2]No tessitura is given because ad libitum repeats; use of musical fragments, etc. preclude any evaluation of this element

[3]Composer suggests that the scores which are "graphic (as are all written scores) but pictorially metaphrastic as well" be interpreted with imagination

POWER TO RISE, THE

Composer: Gordon Johnson Author: Michael Hickaday

Publisher: Marks  No. 4563  Price: 35¢

Voicing: SATB div.;[1] SAT soloists  Grade: med.  Time: 2:00

Accompaniment: piano (organ score available)

Type of Text: secular; humanistic; hope for future

Range and Tessitura:

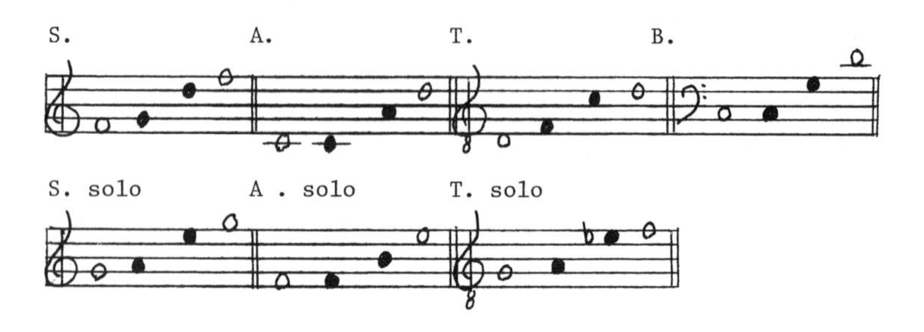


Avant-garde:

written-out tone clusters[2]

Traditional:

Melody: tonal; both conjunct and disjunct passages

Harmony: repeated progressions in ostinato style; altered, augmented, diminished, added tones create wide variety of chords; varying degrees of dissonance

Rhythm: changing meters (3/2, 4/4, 2/4, 3/4); triplet eighths; combinations of eighths and sixteenths

---

[1]Large SATB and small SATB choirs, no divisi within choirs; choirs combined to form "high" and "low" choirs

[2]Written for twelve mixed groups; cluster formed by adding a pitch at a time

PRAISE TO GOD

Composer: Knut Nystedt  Author: Anna L. Barbauld

Publisher: Associated No. A-597 Price: 35¢

Voicing: SATB div.[1] Grade: diff. Time:

Accompaniment: a cappella[2]

Type of Text: sacred; praising

Range and Tessitura:

Avant-garde:

tone clusters; cluster melody graphically notated; rhythmic speech; whispering; glissandos

Traditional:

Melody: tonal; chromatic; augmented octaves; disjunct in places

Harmony: nonfunctional in traditional sense; repetitions of progressions give some functional feeling; unisons; chords built in fourths; major/minor seconds between adjacent voices; many altered chords

Rhythm: changing meters (2/2, 3/2, 4/2, 5/2, 4/4); syncopation; cross rhythms; triplet eighths, halfs

---

[1]Soprano and alto divided into three parts (all perform same melody, but enter in canon-like fashion)

[2]No reduction of voice parts

PRAISE YE HIM

Composer: Ted Nichols Author: biblical

Publisher: Flammer No. A-5579 Price: 30¢

Voicing: SATB div. Grade: med-diff. Time: 3:30

Accompaniment: organ; trumpets, trombones, percussion optional; chimes

Type of Text: sacred; Psalm 150

Range and Tessitura:

Avant-garde:

musical fragments; ad libitum tempo, entrances

Traditional:

Melody: tonal; chromatic occasionally; conjunct

Harmony: nonfunctional, though repeated progressions give some sense of functional movement; close harmonies: sevenths, ninths; seconds and fourths between adjacent voices frequent

Rhythm: changing meters (3/4, 6/8, 2/4, 9/8, 7/8, 2/8, 4/4, 5/4); polyrhythmic section with 4/4, 2/4, 6/4, 7/4, 5/4 combined (each section has its own rhythm and melody, groups from the section enter ad libitum until the whole choir is singing)

PRELUDE AND DANCE FOR VOICES AND HANDS

Composer: Lloyd Pfautsch Author:

Publisher: C. Fischer No. CM 7803 Price: 40¢

Voicing: SATB Grade: med. Time:

Accompaniment: a cappella[1]

Type of Text: syllables, vowels, consonants

Range and Tessitura: relative to individual singers

Avant-garde:

rhythmic speech; inflected rhythmic speech; audible breathing; tongue clicks; lip pops; whispering; glissandos; shouts; hand slaps[2]

Traditional:

Rhythm: triplet eighths; combinations of eighths and sixteenths; syncopation

[1]No reduction of voice parts

[2]Choir performs a variety of hand slaps as a rhythmic accompaniment

PROLOGUE FOR AN UNWRITTEN PLAY

Composer: Jack Boyd  Author: Stephen Crane

Publisher: Warner  No. WB 232  Price: 40¢

Voicing: SATB div.  Grade: med.  Time:

Accompaniment: B♭ clarinet; orchestra chimes (or hand bells); piano[1]

Type of Text: secular; stage directions for setting of a play

Range and Tessitura:

Avant-garde:

speaking; inflected rhythmic speech; ad libitum use of text; whispering; glissandos; finger snaps

Traditional:

Melody: tonal; shifting tonal centers; chromatic

Harmony: functional in a modern idiom; major/minor seconds between adjacent voices; chords with no thirds, fifths; unisons

Rhythm: changing meters (4/4, 3/4); syncopation; triplet eighths, sixteenths; combinations of eighths and sixteenths

---

[1]No reduction of voice parts

PROPHECY OF JOEL, THE

Composer: Eugene Butler  Author: biblical

Publisher: C. Fischer  No. CM 7789  Price: 35¢

Voicing: SATB div.  Grade: med.  Time: 3:00

Accompaniment: organ[1]

Type of Text: sacred; prophetic; praising

Range and Tessitura:

Avant-garde:

inflected rhythmic speech; glissandos

Traditional:

Melody: tonal; chromatic; conjunct

Harmony: triadic; open fifths, octaves; parallel motion of open fifths, fourths

Rhythm: syncopation; triplet eighths; two-against-three; three-against-four; combinations of eighths and sixteenths; much unison rhythmic movement

---

[1]Piano part frequently independent of voice parts

PROPHETIC LAMENT

Composer: Sidney B. Johnson Author: Sidney B. Johnson
Publisher: Pallma No. ED. PC 793 Price: 35¢
Voicing: SATB, s. solo[1] Grade: diff. Time:
Accompaniment: a cappella
Type of Text: sacred; prayer for savior's coming
Range and Tessitura:

Avant-garde:

glissandos; inflected rhythmic speech; rhythmic speech and singing combined; whispering; rubbing hands together

Traditional:

Melody: nontonal; chromatic; augmented, diminished intervals of all types; some repetition of melodic patterns; disjunct at times

Harmony: nonfunctional; long pedal points for basses

Rhythm: syncopation; triplet eighths; combinations of eighths and sixteenths

PSALM 13

Composer: Karl Korte Author: biblical
Publisher: E. C. Schirmer No. 2926 Price: 55¢
Voicing: SATB Grade: diff. Time:
Accompaniment: electronic tape
Type of Text: sacred; petition for God's help

Range and Tessitura:

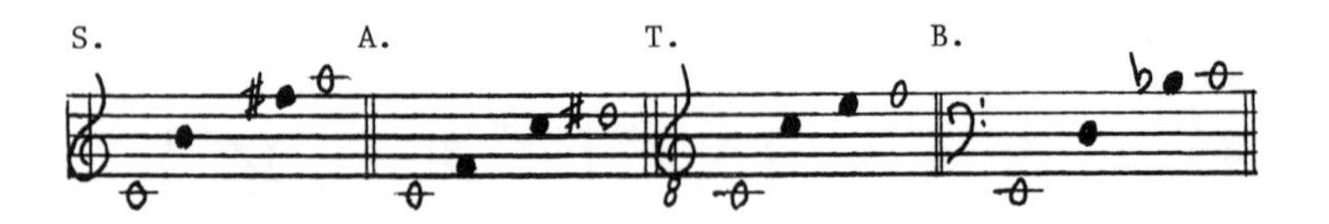


Avant-garde:

ad libitum tempo, use of text; speaking

Traditional:

Melody: nontonal; chromatic; disjunct

Harmony: nonfunctional; open fifths; chords with added tones; parallel sevenths between adjacent voices; diminished or augmented octaves

Rhythm: changing meters (4/4, 2/4, 3/4, 7/8); syncopation; triplet quarters, eighths; combinations of eighths and sixteenths; unison rhythmic movement common

PSALM 27

Composer: Robert Karlén    Author: biblical

Publisher: AMSI    No. AMS 160    Price: 40¢

Voicing: SATB[1]    Grade: med.    Time:

Accompaniment: flute, snare drum, bongos; woodblock, tom-tom[2]

Type of Text: sacred; Latin (no translation with score); praise God

Range and Tessitura:

Avant-garde:

rhythmic speech; rhythmic speech and singing combined

Traditional:

Melody: tonal; shifting tonalities; ostinato melodies; disjunct

Harmony: functional through repetition of patterns; parallel octaves, fourths; chords built in fourths; cross voices

Rhythm: changing meters (5/8, 3/4, 6/8, 2/4, 5/4, 7/8, 4/4) a kind of free alternation of groups of twos and threes is achieved; at times composer directs that no accent is to be used

---

[1]Sopranos have a three-part chord, also divisi in one passage

[2]No reduction of voice parts

PSALM 77

Composer: Knut Nystedt   Author: biblical

Publisher: Walton   No. 2923   Price: 50¢

Voicing: SATB div; SATB soloists   Grade: diff.   Time: 8:00

Accompaniment: a cappella[1]

Type of Text: sacred; confidence in God

Range and Tessitura:

Avant-garde:

rhythmic speech; glissandos; moaning; whispering

Traditional:

Melody: tonal; chromatic; disjunct; augmented and diminished intervals

Harmony: sevenths, ninths; open fifths; major/minor seconds, fourths between adjacent voices with parallel motion

Rhythm: changing meters (2/2, 3/2, 4/2); triplet quarters, halfs; syncopation

[1]No reduction of voice parts

PSALM 100

Composer: John Carter Author: biblical

Publisher: Walton No. 2932 Price: 40¢

Voicing: mixed voices[1] Grade: med. Time:

Accompaniment: a cappella[2]

Type of Text: sacred; praising

Range and Tessitura:

Avant-garde:

rhythmic speech; tone clusters; cluster melodies; ad libitum tempo; rhythmic speech and singing together; improvise melody; humming; glissandos; graphic notation of rhythm

Traditional:

Melody: modal; recitation on single pitch

Harmony: chords built in seconds, sevenths

Rhythm: unmetered; syncopation; triplet eighths, quarters; eighth note pulse grouped in threes and fours

---

[1]Four choirs with men and women's voices in each; each group in unison

[2]No reduction of voice parts

PSALM 139

Composer: Carlton Young | Author: biblical

Publisher: Hope | No. CY 3332 | Price: 30¢

Voicing: SATB; solo voice[1] | Grade: med-easy | Time:

Accompaniment: oboe;[2] organ may be used to double voice parts

Type of Text: sacred; confidence before God

Range and Tessitura:

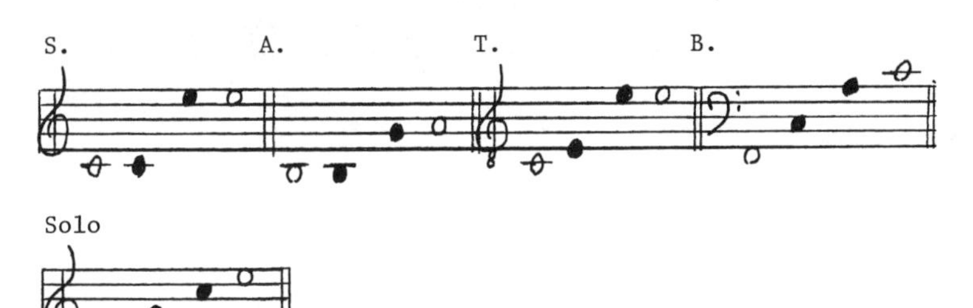


Avant-garde:

whispering; speaking; ad libitum use of text

Traditional:

Melody: tonal; some chromatics

Harmony: tonal; sevenths; chords with added tones; pedal point in bass; major/minor seconds between adjacent voices

Rhythm: unmetered; traditional notation used; quarter note pulse for measures of varying lengths

---

[1]Congregation or audience participation desired

[2]Oboeist must improvise on supplied pitches

PSALM FOR TODAY

Composer: Buryl Red Author: Ed. Seabough

Publisher: Broadman No. Price:

Voicing: SATB Grade: med-easy Time:

Accompaniment: piano, electronic tape - optional

Type of Text: sacred

Range and Tessitura:

Avant-garde:

inflected rhythmic speech; spoken glissandos

Traditional:

Melody: tonal; occasional chromatic; scale and chord patterns

Harmony: functional; unisons, two-parts; sevenths

Rhythm: changing meters (4/4, 2/4, 3/4, 3/2, 3/8); syncopation; triplet quarters

PSALM OF PRAISE[1]

Composer: James D. Cram Author: biblical

Publisher: Flammer No. B-5157 Price: 35¢
Voicing: SSAA or SSAATTBB[2] Grade: med. Time: 5:00
Accompaniment: piano (organ)[3]
Type of Text: sacred; praising God's love, constancy, goodness
Range and Tessitura:[4]

Avant-garde:

rhythmic speech; glissandos

Traditional:

Melody: tonal; chromatics; conjunct

Harmony: functional; frequent modulations; altered chords; major/minor seconds between adjacent voices

Rhythm: changing meters (3/4, 4/4, 2/4, 5/4); syncopation; triplet eighths; combinations of eighths and sixteenths; shifting accents

---

[1]Three separate compositions; probably could be performed separately

[2]Special instructions for mixed choir

[3]Some facility needed; needs to read accidentals; second composition is a cappella

[4]Choral parts in treble clefs throughout

PSHELLEY'S PSALM

Composer: Richard Felciano Author: Shelley Hischier

Publisher: E. C. Schirmer    No. 2920    Price:

Voicing: SATB    Grade: diff.    Time: 1:20

Accompaniment: a cappella[1]

Type of Text: sacred/secular; serious novelty

Range and Tessitura:

Avant-garde:

glissandos; clapping; shouts; rhythmic speech; fragmentation of words; graphic notation of dynamics; ad libitum pitch; choreography

Traditional:

Melody: tonal; isolated fragments; beginning pitches have to be "heard" or picked up from the preceding pitch (not always easy)

Harmony: nonfunctional; major/minor seconds between adjacent voices, almost form tone clusters at times

Rhythm: syncopation; combinations of eighths and sixteenths; fragments of "rhythms"

[1]No reduction of voice parts

RECONCILIATION

Composer: Lloyd Pfautsch    Author: biblical

Publisher: Abingdon    No. APM-345    Price: 35¢

Voicing: SATB div.    Grade: med.    Time:

Accompaniment: a cappella with trumpet obligato (required)[1]

Type of Text: sacred; praising Christ as redeemer

Range and Tessitura:

Avant-garde:

inflected rhythmic speech

Traditional:

Melody: tonal; conjunct or triadic patterns

Harmony: functional; major seconds (as passing tones) between adjacent voices

Rhythm: changing meters (3/4, 4/4); syncopation; combinations of eighths and sixteenths

---

[1]No reduction of voice parts

REJOICE, THIS IS THE DAY

Composer: F. Dale Bengtson Author: biblical

Publisher: Gentry No. G-174 Price: 30¢

Voicing: two-part Grade: easy Time: 1:00

Accompaniment: a cappella

Type of Text: sacred; praising

Range and Tessitura: not applicable

Avant-garde:

inflected rhythmic speech; glissandos; ad libitum use of text; modification of sound with hands

Traditional:

Rhythm: changing meters (3/4, 4/4, 2/4)

RESERVOIR

Composer: Robert Morris
Author:
Publisher: Walton
No. 2914
Price: $1.00
Voicing: SATB, div.[1]
Grade: med.
Time: 5:00
Accompaniment: a cappella
Type of Text: novelty; vowels, consonants (glossary of sounds supplied)
Range and Tessitura: not applicable
Avant-garde:

graphic notation of pitch, rhythm; improvisation; glissandos; lip flapping; rolled "R"; ad libitum use of musical fragments (events), rhythm; finger snaps; whistling; humming; tongue clicks; sighs; laughing (giggling); speaking

Traditional: not applicable

[1]Each part is divided into four sub-sections

RISING SUN, THE[1]

Composer: Frank Pooler & Brent Pierce
Author: Japanese Haiku
Publisher: Somerset
No. CE 4328
Price: 75¢
Voicing: SATB div; ST soloists[2]
Grade: med.
Time:
Accompaniment: piano; four chromatic pitch pipes; Jew's harp; güiro; educator bells; bell lyre; wind chimes
Type of Text: secular; mood pictures
Range and Tessitura:

Avant-garde:

inflected rhythmic speech; vibrato; graphic notation of pitch, rhythm, dynamics; glissandos; murmuring; whispering; unvoiced sounds; vibrating lips; flutter tongue; tone clusters tongue clicks; glottal stroke; ad libitum rhythm

Traditional:

Melody: conjunct; some isolated pitches; ostinato-type melodies

Harmony: nonfunctional; ostinato; minor seconds between adjacent voices

Rhythm: traditional notation as well as nontraditional; triplet eighths, quarters; polyrhythms (one, two, three, and four pulses combined); syncopation

---

[1]Set of ten short compositions using a variety of voicings, accompaniments, idioms

[2]Soloists improvise in several compositions

[3]Low notes in unison with bass

ROLL CALL

Composer: Arthur Frackenpohl Author:

Publisher: Plymouth No. PCS-528 Price: 35¢

Voicing: two-part Grade: easy Time:

Accompaniment: triangle; wood block; rhythm sticks; drum (other percussion possible)

Type of Text: secular; names of States

Range and Tessitura: not applicable

Avant-garde:

rhythmic speech; finger snaps; hand claps; thigh slaps; foot stamping

Traditional:

Rhythm: changing meters (2/4, 4/4); syncopation; triplet eighths; two-against-three

RONDES

Composer: Folke Rabe
Author:
Publisher: Hansen
No. 11894
Price: 35¢
Voicing: SATB
Grade: diff.
Time: 2:45
Accompaniment: a cappella
Type of Text: syllables, vowels, consonants; international phonetics
Range and Tessitura: relative to individual

Avant-garde:

graphic notation of pitch, rhythm; ad libitum entrances, use of text, pitch, rhythm; improvisational in style throughout

Traditional:

Melody: occasional pitch indicated (pitch pipe recommended)

Harmony: aleatoric

Rhythm: occasional group of eighths, sixteenths notated

"ƨSƨ"

Composer: Emmett Yoshioka
Author: Emmett Yoshioka
Publisher: Walton
No. 2918
Price: 50¢
Voicing: SATB;[1] SATB soloists
Grade: diff.
Time:
Accompaniment: a cappella
Type of Text: secular; explores "s" sounding words
Range and Tessitura: relative to individual singers

Avant-garde:

ad libitum pitch, entrances (by conductor); glissandos and portamentos; glissandos with vibrato; sustaining of consonants of words; traditional rhythmic symbols used but with only approximate durational meaning

Traditional: not applicable

[1]Sixteen-part choir; each section subdivided into four

SACRED HAIR

Composer: Edwin London    Author: biblical

Publisher: Boonin    No. B 168    Price: 90¢

Voicing: SATB div.    Grade: diff.    Time: 8:00

Accompaniment: 4 combs (actual pitches notated to be hummed); organ

Type of Text: sacred; Gen. 27:11, Job 4:15-17; holiness of God

Range and Tessitura:

Avant-garde:

ad libitum rhythm; graphic notation of rhythm; tone clusters; glissandos; vibrato

Traditional:

Melody: tonal, nontonal; disjunct; chromatics; augmented, diminished intervals

Harmony: two contrasting styles; (1) tonal, functional, though altered chords frequent; (2) nontonal, nonfunctional; fourths, fifths; major/minor seconds between adjacent voices.

Rhythm: changing meters (3/2, 4/4, 3/4, 5/4, 4/2); syncopation; triplet quarters

SACRED SERVICE, A

Composer: Max DiJulio Author:

Publisher: Un. of Miami No. UM-123 Price: $1.25

Voicing: SSATB Grade: diff. Time: 12:00

Accompaniment: electric guitar;[1] piano, organ or harpsichord can substitute

Type of Text: sacred; Latin; liturgical

Range and Tessitura:

Avant-garde:

rhythmic speech and singing combined

Traditional:

Melody: tonal; chromatic

Harmony: functional; sevenths, ninths; altered chords; chords with added tones

Rhythm: changing meters (4/4, 3/4, 5/4, 7/8, 3/8, 2/4); syncopation; triplet quarters

[1]Classical guitar techniques needed; part edited by Johnny Smith

SANCTUS

Composer: Lawrence Widdoes Author:

Publisher: Presser No. 312-41123 Price: 75¢

Voicing: SATB div.[1] Grade: diff. Time:

Accompaniment: piano,[2] woodblock

Type of Text: sacred; Latin "sanctus," English comment about worship

Range and Tessitura:

Avant-garde:

sustaining and repetition of vowel, consonant sounds; declamatory speech; speech and singing combined; mumbling; whispering; glissandos; whistling; flutter tongue; improvise text; ad libitum pitch

Traditional:

Melody: nontonal; chromatic; conjunct, disjunct; hearing cues may be difficult at times

Harmony: nonfunctional; major/minor seconds between adjacent voices; close voicing at times

Rhythm: changing meters (4/4, 6/8, 3/4, 5/16, 3/16); triplet eighths, quarters, sixteenths; duplet eighths in 6/8 meter; two-against-three

---

[1]Each section subdivided into five parts on occasion for rhythmic speech passages; all pitched, sung passages straight SATB

[2]No reduction of voice parts

SAUL

Composer: Egil Hovland Author: biblical

Publisher: Walton  No. M-126  Price: $1:00

Voicing: SATB div.; narrator  Grade: diff.  Time:

Accompaniment: organ

Type of Text: sacred; Saul on road to Damascus

Range and Tessitura:

Avant-garde:

ad libitum entrances, tempo; whispering

Traditional:

Melody: nontonal; chromatic; disjunct at times

Harmony: nonfunctional; unison, two-part passages; augmented, diminished octaves between parts; harmonies shifted by movement of one voice

Rhythm: changing meters (4/4, 3/4, 6/4, 5/4); unmetered section with traditional rhythmic symbols; triplet eighths; syncopation

SEPARATION

Composer: Wallace DePue  Author: Sidney B. Johnson

Publisher: Pallma  No. ED. PC 806  Price: 30¢

Voicing: SATB  Grade: diff.  Time:

Accompaniment: a cappella

Type of Text: secular; loneliness

Range and Tessitura:

Avant-garde:

tone clusters; glissandos

Traditional:

Melody: nontonal; chromatic; disjunct

Harmony: nonfunctional; major/minor seconds between adjacent voices and in parallel motion

Rhythm: changing meters (6/4, 3/4); syncopation

## SEVEN LAST DAYS, THE

Composer: Edward Miller  Author: Donald Justice

Publisher: Ione  No. 2906  Price: 50¢

Voicing: SATB  Grade: diff.  Time:

Accompaniment: electronic tape;[1] chimes; wooden wind chimes; marimba; snare drum; suspended cymbal; triangle; 16mm silent film[2]

Type of Text: secular; "moods" of the days of the week

Range and Tessitura:

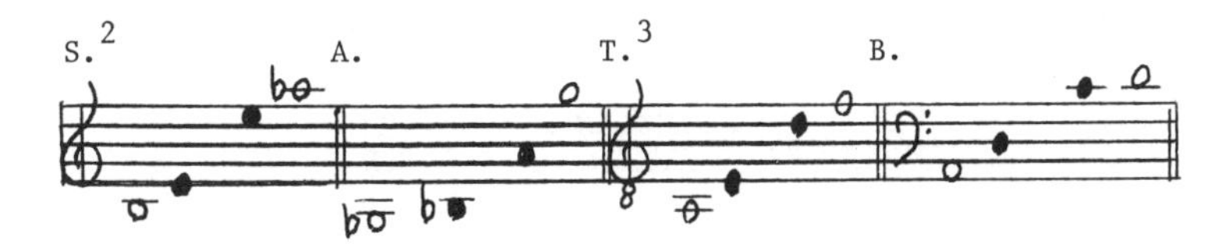


Avant-garde:

rhythmic speech; glissandos; ad libitum pitch; shouting

Traditional:

Melody: tonal; disjunct; intervals of fourth, fifth prominent; shifting tonal centers

Harmony: nonfunctional; open parallel fifths; major/minor seconds between adjacent voices; unison in SA and TB; drone Bass and Tenor

Rhythm: changing meters (3/2, 3/4, 6/8); syncopation

---

[1]Two stereo tapes used; tape and film available

[2]Low notes in unison with Alto

[3]Low notes in unison with Bass

SEVEN LAST WORDS OF CHRIST ON THE CROSS, THE

Composer: Daniel Pinkham Author: biblical

Publisher: E. C. Schirmer No. 2907 Price: 60¢

Voicing: SATB; T, Bar, B-Bar soloists[1] Grade: diff. Time:

Accompaniment: organ; electronic tape[2]

Type of Text: sacred; Christ's passion

Range and Tessitura:

Avant-garde:

choral part entirely traditional in notation; choir sings with electronic tape accompaniment

Traditional:

Melody: nontonal; chromatic; disjunct; augmented, diminished intervals

Harmony: nonfunctional; augmented, diminished octaves, major/minor seconds, sevenths between adjacent voices common

Rhythm: changing meters (3/4, 4/4, 2/4, 7/8, 5/4); triplet eighths, quarters; combinations of eighths and sixteenths

[1]Bass-baritone solo extensive; serves as the evangelist. Tenor and baritone solos short, serve as the two criminals

[2]Tape available

SHELLS

Composer: Knut Nystedt | Author: Kathleen Raine
Publisher: AMP | No. A-715 | Price: 45¢
Voicing: SSAA, div.[1] | Grade: med-diff | Time:

Accompaniment: a cappella

Type of Text: secular/sacred

Range and Tessitura:

Avant-garde:

glissandos; whispering

Traditional:

Melody: tonal; shifting tonality; chromatics

Harmony: ostinatos; chords in fourths; major/minor seconds between adjacent voices

Rhythm: unmetered section; two-against-three; triplet eighths

---

[1]Altos divide into I, II, III to sing a melody canonically

SIC TRANSIT

Composer: Richard Felciano Author: biblical

Publisher: E. C. Schirmer No. 2903 Price: 45¢

Voicing: SAB[1] Grade: med. Time: 1:21

Accompaniment: organ;[2] electronic tape[3]

Type of Text: sacred; Easter

Range and Tessitura:

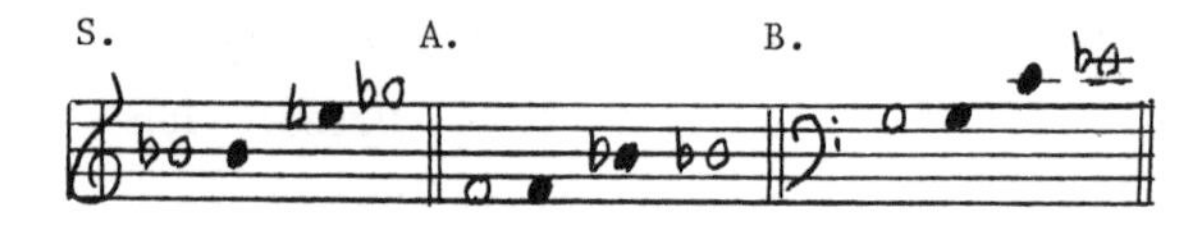


Avant-garde:

ad libitum use of text, entrances; chain reaction of "passing on" a spoken text

Traditional:

Melody: chanting on single pitch; one passage of disjunct melody

Harmony: nonfunctional; ostinato effect

Rhythm: unmetered; traditional symbols used; combinations of eighths and sixteenths

---

[1]SSA arrangement available (#2807)

[2]Organist must improvise; have good rhythmic sense

[3]Tape available

SIGNPOSTS

Composer: Eskil Hemberg  Author: biblical
Publisher: Hansen  No. 11842  Price: 35¢
Voicing: SATB div.  Grade: diff.  Time:
Accompaniment: a cappella
Type of Text: sacred; Psalms; God's rule; God's providence
Range and Tessitura:

Avant-garde:

tone clusters; cluster melody with graphic notation; whispering; sighing; glissandos; improvise melody, rhythm; modification of sound with hands; stage position specified

Traditional:

Melody: tonal; chromatic; conjunct; ostinato figures

Harmony: chords built in seconds, fourths; alternations between major/minor thirds; chords with both major/minor thirds present

Rhythm: syncopation; triplet eighths, quarters, halfs; three-against-four; grace notes

SIGNS

Composer: Richard Felciano  Author:[1]
Publisher: E. C. Schirmer  No. 2927  Price:
Voicing: SATB  Grade: med-easy  Time: 4:48

Accompaniment: electronic tape, 1-3 filmstrips

Type of Text: sacred; prophetic

Range and Tessitura:

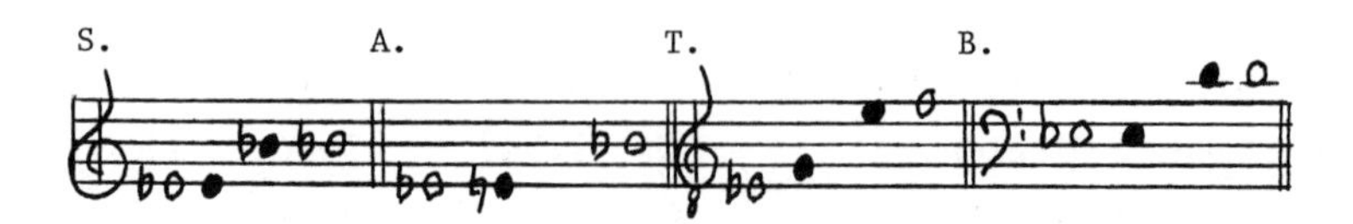


Avant-garde:

rhythmic speech; whispering; musical fragments; shouting; glissandos; special location of performing forces

Traditional:

Melody: tonal; ostinatos; long sustained pitches; minor seconds; chromatics

Harmony: unisons; static harmony; some minor seconds between adjacent voices

Rhythm: triplet sixteenths

---

[1]R. Buckminster Fuller, Pierre Teilhard de Chardin, Jean-François Revel, St. Luke, man

SLUGS

Composer: Sydney Hodkinson Author: Keith Gunderson

Publisher: Merion No. 342-40103 Price: 40¢

Voicing: SATB Grade: med-diff. Time: 1:30

Accompaniment: a cappella[1]

Type of Text: secular; novelty

Range and Tessitura:

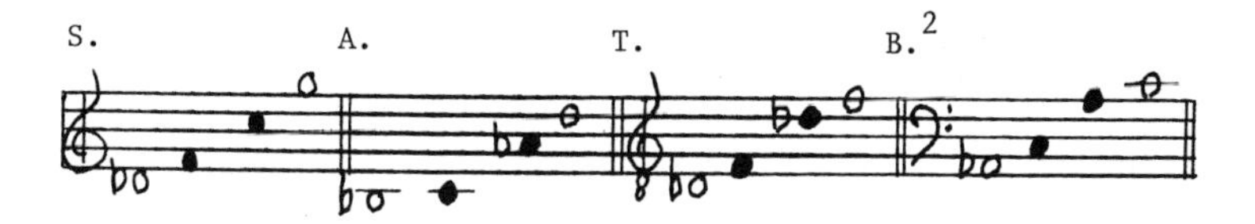


Avant-garde:

glissandos; fragments of syllables

Traditional:

Melody: tonal; shifting tonalities; chromatic; disjunct

Harmony: nonfunctional; major/minor seconds between adjacent voices and in parallel motion

Rhythm: changing meters (4/4, 2/4); syncopation; triplet eighths

[1]No reduction of voice parts

[2]Falsetto "f" required once

SNAIL

Composer: Sydney Hodkinson Author: Keith Gunderson

Publisher: Merion No. 342-40107 Price: 30¢

Voicing: 3 choirs[1] Grade: med-easy Time:

Accompaniment: piano, cymbals - optional

Type of Text: secular

Range and Tessitura:

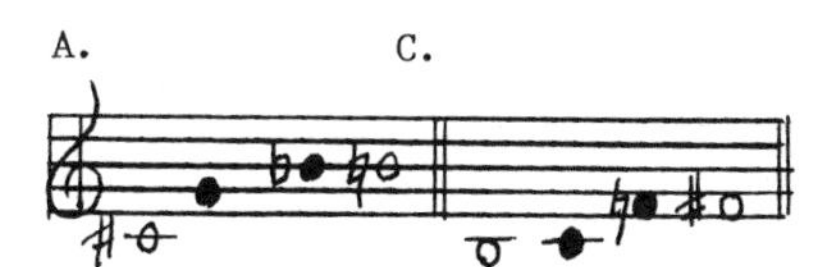

Avant-garde:

tone clusters written out; rhythmic speech; prolongation of vowels, consonants of words

Traditional:

Melody: nontonal; conjunct; chromatics

Harmony: tone clusters built by adding one pitch at a time, chord then altered by shifting one pitch at a time

Rhythm: syncopation

[1] Group A: solo or two to four female voices; perform the melody of the composition; Group B: small group of mixed voices performs only rhythmic speech; Group C: large group of mixed voices perform five-part tone clusters

SOLITUDE OF SPACE

Composer: Brent Pierce Author: Emily Dickinson

Publisher: Walton No. 2978 Price: 45¢

Voicing: SATB div. Grade: med. Time:

Accompaniment: piano[1]

Type of Text: secular/sacred; kinds of solitude

Range and Tessitura:

Avant-garde:

tone clusters (written out, built by adding tones); choreography (hands, head movements)

Traditional:

Melody: tonal; some chromatics; disjunct in places

Harmony: functional; unisons; major/minor seconds, fourths, fifths, augmented, diminished intervals between adjacent voices; seventh, ninth, eleventh chords

Rhythm: much unison rhythmic movement

---

[1]Piano part totally independent of voices; no reduction of voice parts

SOME BRIGHT STARS FOR QUEEN'S COLLEGE

Composer: David Bedford Author:

Publisher: Universal No. 15359 Price: 50¢

Voicing: four groups Grade: easy Time: 3:00

Accompaniment: two alto melodicas; piano; three recorders; other instruments - optional

Type of Text: secular; names of stars

Range and Tessitura: relative to individual singer

Avant-garde:

graphic notation of pitch, rhythm; time segments in seconds; chest thumping; glissandos; lip tremulo

Traditional: not applicable

SONG OF DANIEL

Composer: Eugene Butler Author: biblical

Publisher: C. Fischer No. CM 7766 Price: 30¢

Voicing: SATB div. Grade: med-easy Time: 3:40

Accompaniment: piano or organ; tambourine; woodblock; cymbal - optional

Type of Text: sacred; praising

Range and Tessitura:

Avant-garde:

rhythmic speech

Traditional:

Melody: tonal; scale, chord patterns; shifting tonalities

Harmony: functional; chords with added tones; major/minor seconds between adjacent voices; doubling of parts between men and women voices

Rhythm: changing meters (4/4, 5/4, 2/4); triplet eighths, quarters; syncopation; cross rhythms between choir and accompaniment

## SONGS FROM EMILY[1]

Composer: Allyson Brown Author: Emily Dickinson

Publisher: Shawnee No. E-177 Price: 50¢

Voicing: SA Grade: med. Time:

Accompaniment: piano;[2] tambourine; bongos; finger cymbals

Type of Text: secular; variety of moods

Range and Tessitura:

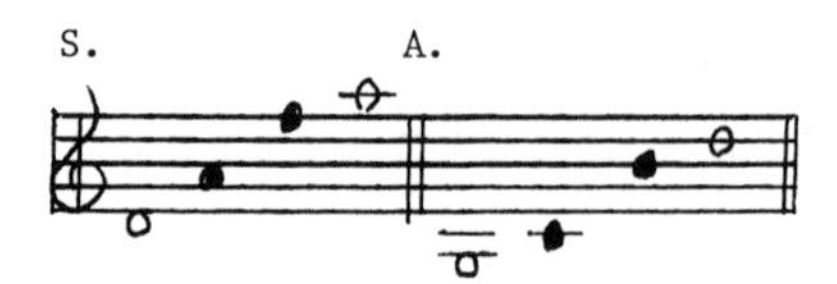

Avant-garde:

graphic notation of rhythm

Traditional:

Melody: tonal; chromatic; conjunct though intervals of fourth and fifth occur with some frequency; ostinato patterns

Harmony: functional; intervals of every type between the two voices; sevenths, ninths prominent

Rhythm: changing meters (4/4, 2/4, 3/4, 5/4); triplet quarters; much unison rhythmic movement; second composition uses graphic notation of rhythm; others completely traditional

---

[1]Suite of four compositions; probably can be performed separately

[2]Pianist needs some facility, especially in reading accidentals

SORCERER, THE[1]

Composer: Merrill Ellis Author: Robert Lockwood

Publisher: Shawnee No. A-1213 Price: $1.50

Voicing: SATB; Bar. soloist[2] Grade: med-easy Time: 15:55

Accompaniment: electronic tape;[3] color slides;[3] optional band: piccolo, clarinet, 2 trumpets, trombone, snare drum, bass drum, cymbals

Type of Text: secular; fairy tale

Range and Tessitura:

Avant-garde:

graphic notation of pitch, rhythm, dynamics; tongue clicks; whistling; clapping; finger snaps; whispering; ad libitum pitch, rhythm, entrances, tempo, use of text; choreography

Traditional:

Melody: tonal; conjunct

Harmony: functional; unison passages; occasional diminished octave between adjacent voices

Rhythm: unmetered sections; changing meters (3/4, 4/4, 2/4); triplet quarters; syncopation

---

[1]A stage drama for baritone soloist, chorus, and tape

[2]Role long, rather difficult; needs acting ability

[3]Tape - $10.00; set of slides (20 35mm) - $10.00

SOUND AND FURY

| Composer: Jean Britton | Author: | |
|---|---|---|
| Publisher: Elkan-Vogel | No. 362-03147 | Price: 30¢ |
| Voicing: SA | Grade: med-easy | Time: |

Accompaniment: a cappella

Type of Text: secular; Declaration of Independence; consonants only

Range and Tessitura:

Avant-garde:

fragments of syllables; glissandos; rhythmic speech; rhythmic speech and singing combined

Traditional:

Melody: tonal; chromatics; diminished, augmented fourths

Harmony: unison; pedal points

Rhythm: syncopation; combinations of eighths and sixteenths

[1]Lowest pitches sung in unison with Alto part

SOUND PATTERNS

Composer: Pauline Oliveros Author:

Publisher: Boonin No. B. 111 Price: 50¢

Voicing: SATB Grade: diff. Time:

Accompaniment: a cappella[1]

Type of Text: syllables, vowels, consonants

Range and Tessitura: not applicable

Avant-garde:

whispering; heavy aspirations; lip pops; tongue clicks; modification of sound with hands; finger snaps; graphic notation of pitch; glottal stop; glissandos; ad libitum rhythm

Traditional:

Rhythm: changing meters (4/4, 3/4, 1/4); syncopation; triplet eighths, sixteenths, thirty-seconds; combinations of eighths and sixteenths

[1]No reduction of voice parts

SOUND PATTERNS I

Composer: Bernard Rands    Author:

Publisher: Universal    No. 14647    Price: 50¢

Voicing: four equal groups    Grade: easy    Time:

Accompaniment: a cappella

Type of Text: secular; novelty; nursery rhymes

Range and Tessitura: relative to individual singers

Avant-garde:

whispering; tone cluster; tongue clicks; graphic notation of pitch; trilled"R"; hand clapping; finger snapping; unvoiced sounds; ad libitum rhythm; whistling

Traditional: not applicable

SOUND PATTERNS 2

Composer: Bernard Rands    Author:

Publisher: Universal    No. 14651    Price: 50¢

Voicing: Unison    Grade: med. easy    Time:

Accompaniment: percussion, string, melody instruments[1]

Type of Text: consonant sounds

Range and Tessitura: not applicable

Avant-garde:

clapping; finger snaps; humming; shouting; graphic notation

of pitch, rhythm; time segments; ad libitum entrances, durations; unvoiced sounds; tongue clicks

Traditional: not applicable

---

[1]Score calls for six groups of instruments; any or all of the following instruments can be used: glockenspiels, metallophones, tubular bells, triangles, finger cymbals, chime bars, suspended cymbals, jingles, tambourines, claves, castanets, maracas, xylophones, melodicas, harmonicas, guitars, auto harps, other instruments which can interpret traditional notation literally

## SOUND PATTERNS 3[1]

Composer: Bernard Rands Author:

Publisher: Universal No. 15348 Price: 65¢

Voicing: any Grade: easy Time:

Accompaniment: a cappella

Type of Text: syllables, vowels, consonants

Range and Tessitura: relative to individual singers

Avant-garde:

ad libitum text; graphic notation of pitch, rhythm; unvoiced sounds; tongue clicks; finger snaps; clapping; humming; time segments

Traditional: not applicable

---

[1]A class project to develop awareness of sound possibilities

## SOUND PATTERNS 4

Composer: Bernard Rands Author:

Publisher: Universal No. 15349 Price: 50¢

Voicing: unspecified Grade: easy Time:

Accompaniment: three groups of instruments suggested: metal percussion, wood percussion, melody instruments; performers urged to use any instruments which can interpret the graphic score

Type of Text: not applicable

Range and Tessitura: relative to individual singer

Avant-garde:

graphic notation of pitch, rhythm; music cells or fragments in nontraditional notation to be interpreted by performers as they see fit; ad libitum interpretation of directions, notations

Traditional: not applicable

SOUND PIECES

Composer: Allen Brings Author: David S. Walker

Publisher: Shawnee No. E-154 Price: 45¢

Voicing: SATB[1] Grade: easy Time:[2]

Accompaniment: any percussion instruments; kitchen utensils; electronic mixer desirable

Type of Text: secular; novelty

Range and Tessitura: relative to individual singers

Avant-garde:

glissandos; whispering; whistling; tone clusters (written out); rhythmic speech; graphic notation of pitch, rhythm, dynamics; shouting; rolled "R"

Traditional:

Rhythm: syncopation; triplet sixteenths

SPACE-DRAGON OF GALATAR, THE

Composer: John Paynter Author: Paul Townsend

Publisher: Universal No. 15506 Price:

Voicing: SSA (unchanged)[1] Grade: med. Time:

Accompaniment: piano;[2] cymbal; optional percussion; electronic tape (to be made by group)

Type of Text: secular; opera for children; fairy-tale

Range and Tessitura:

Avant-garde:

vocal sound effects; glissandos; "roar"; graphic notation of pitch

Traditional:

Melody: tonal; modal; chromatics

Harmony: major/minor thirds; pedal points

Rhythm: changing meters (4/4, 2/4, 8/8, 9/8, 6/8, 7/8); triplet eighths; two-against-three; three-against-two; combinations of eighths and sixteenths

---

[1]Three groups of singer-actors; most of singing by single groups; only occasional two- or three-part passages

[2]Pianist needs some facility; be strong rhythmically; vamping; improvisation on materials supplied; must read accidentals

SPEAK WORDS OF PRAISE

Composer: F. Dale Bengtson Author: biblical

Publisher: Gentry No. G-156 Price: 30¢

Voicing: SATB Grade: easy Time:

Accompaniment: optional tom-tom

Type of Text: sacred; Latin; Gloria in excelsis Deo

Range and Tessitura:

Avant-garde:

rhythmic speech; improvisation on text

Traditional:

Melody: short modal scale passages

Harmony: minor chords

Rhythm: changing meters (3/4, 4/4); triplet eighths

SUN, THE SOARING EAGLE, THE TURQUOISE PRINCE, THE GOD, THE

Composer: William Bergsma Author: Bernardino de Sahagun

Publisher: Galaxy No. GMC 2428 Price: $3.50

Voicing: SATB div; speaking chorus Grade: diff. Time: 10:00

Accompaniment: three possibilities: 1) 2 B♭ trumpets, tenor trombone, bass trombone, tuba, 3 bongos, maracas, wood-block, whip, ratchet, triangle, suspended cymbal, snare, tenor and bass drums, glockenspiel, xylophone, vibraphone, whistle; 2) piano and the percussion mentioned above; 3) piano alone[1]

Type of Text: secular; Aztec civilization

Range and Tessitura:

Avant-garde:

rhythmic speech; inflected rhythmic speech; shouting; ad libitum use of text; spoken glissandos; whistling; rhythmic speech and singing combined

Traditional:

Melody: tonal; shifting tonalities; chromatic; fourths; repetition of melodic figures

Harmony: functional, nonfunctional; repetitions of progressions; chords built in fourths; fourths, seconds between adjacent voices; unisons; altered chords; parallel fourths frequent

Rhythm: changing meters (4/4, 3/4, 2/4, 5/4, 3/2, 5/8, 9/8, 6/4); triplet quarters, eighths; three-against-two; syncopation; combinations of eighths and sixteenths; unison rhythmic movement

[1]Pianist needs facility; no reduction of voice parts

SUONI (SOUNDS)

Composer: Knut Nystedt    Author:

Publisher: AMP    No. A-679    Price: 45¢

Voicing: SA div.[1]    Grade: med-diff.    Time: 8:00

Accompaniment: flute; marimba required[2]

Type of Text: syllables, vowels

Range and Tessitura:

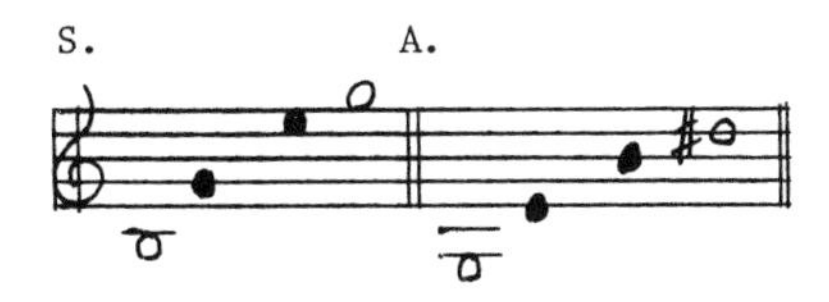


Avant-garde:

glissandos; tone clusters (gradually built up); whispering;

glissandoes on "r"; wide vibrato; vibrating lips, tongue; ad libitum pitch; inflected rhythmic speech

Traditional:

Melody: tone row; augmented fourths, fifths, sixths; chromatic

Harmony: nonfunctional; chords built up by adding pitches; ostinato-type harmonic movement

Rhythm: changing meters (4/4, 3/4, 2/4, 9/8, 12/8 appear in accompaniment while 3/4, 4/4 appear in the voices); syncopation; cross rhythms between accompaniment and voices

---

[1]Division into six parts for tone clusters

[2]Facility required for both instrumental parts; totally independent of voice parts

SURELY THE LORD IS IN THIS PLACE

Composer: David Stocker Author:

Publisher: Agape No. AG 7203 Price: 35¢

Voicing: SATB-speaking choir Grade: easy Time:

Accompaniment: percussion - optional

Type of Text: sacred; the House of God

Range and Tessitura: not applicable

Avant-garde:

rhythmic speech

Traditional: not applicable

SYNTHESIZER, THE

Composer: Maurice Gardner Author:

Publisher: Staff No. 657 Price: 30¢

Voicing: SATB Grade: easy Time: 2:00

Accompaniment: piano; metronome

Type of Text: secular; novelty

Range and Tessitura:

Avant-garde:

glissandos; shouting

Traditional:

Melody: tonal; some chromaticism; repetition of patterns

Harmony: unison, two-part; tonal; passage of chromatic harmonies

Rhythm: syncopation

TAKE A SHAPE

Composer: George Self Author: Oxford Dictionary

Publisher: Universal No. UE 15397 Price: 65¢

Voicing: unspecified[1]

Accompaniment: any instruments[1]

Type of Text: secular; novelty

Range and Tessitura: relative to individual singer

Avant-garde:

whispering; speaking; graphic notation of pitch, rhythm; ad libitum interpretation of undefined sighs; rolled "R"; whistling; barking

Traditional:

Rhythm: time segments (basically 4/4); triplet eighths; syncopation; combinations of eighths and sixteenths

---

[1]A class project where students work out what they want in the composition within certain guidelines supplied by the composer

TANGENTS V

Composer: Hanley Jackson Author:

Publisher: Shawnee No. A-1277 Price: 35¢

Voicing: SATB div.; T. solo[1] Grade: med. Time: 4:15

Accompaniment: electronic tape[2]

Type of Text: vowels, consonants

Range and Tessitura:

Avant-garde:

wide, slow vibrato; ad libitum talking, whispering, laughing; approximate pitch; glissandos; foot stomping

Traditional:

Melody: long sustained notes; conjunct; (pitches supplied by tape)

Harmony: built from unisons, octaves; nonfunctional; sevenths, seconds between adjacent voices

Rhythm: changing meters (4/4, 6/4); combinations of eighths and sixteenths; triplet eighths, sixteenths; no stress desired

---

[1]Tenor solo only one measure

[2]Tape available - $6.00; no reduction of voice parts

TEMA

Composer: Alfred Janson    Author:

Publisher: Walton    No. M115    Price: $1.00

Voicing: three-part women/men, div.[1]    Grade: diff.    Time:

Accompaniment: organ (pedals necessary); vibraphone; tam-tam; snare drum; piano[2]

Type of Text: vowels

Range and Tessitura:

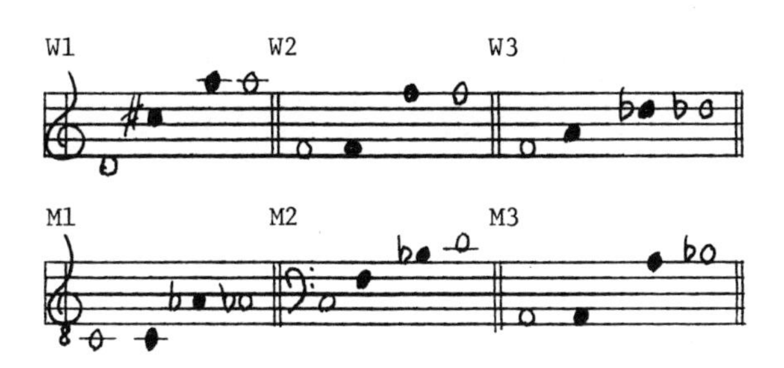


Avant-garde:

ad libitum whispering, talking (no text supplied); talking, whispering combined with singing; glissandos

Traditional:

Melody: tonal; long sustained pitches; chromatic; conjunct; repetition of patterns

Harmony: nonfunctional; shifting (chord changes achieved by one voice moving while others remain stationary); major/minor seconds, sevenths between adjacent voices

Rhythm: syncopation; each voice part independent; unmetered section

---

[1]Twelve independent voice parts; high, medium, low voices divisi for women; high, medium, low voices divisi for men

[2]Pianist needs facility in reading accidentals, playing widely spaced chords, pedaling

THERZACAT BOOGIE

Composer: Sydney Hodkinson Author: Keith Gunderson

Publisher: Merion No. 342-40109 Price: 40¢

Voicing: three-part[1] Grade: med. Time:

Accompaniment: piano; percussion suggested - optional

Type of Text: secular; novelty

Range and Tessitura:

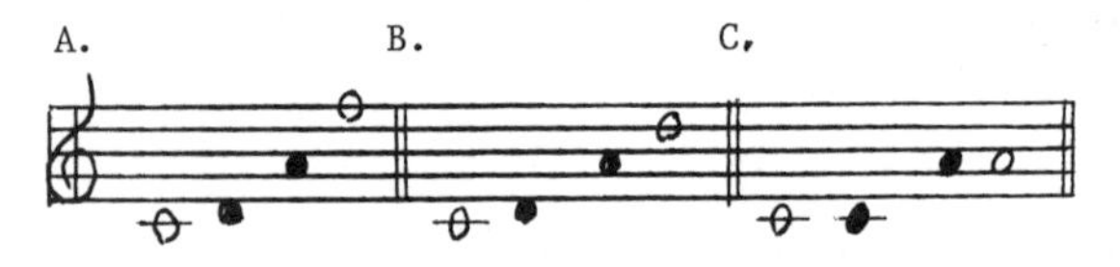


Avant-garde:

finger snaps; glissandos; whispering

Traditional:

Melody: tonal; voice crossings; conjunct; intervals of fourth, fifth

Harmony: functional through repetition of patterns; major/minor seconds between adjacent voices; very close voicing

Rhythm: syncopation; dotted eighth and sixteenth rhythms

[1]High, medium and low voices

THOUGH IT SHIVERS

Composer: Sydney Hodkinson Author: Keith Gunderson

Publisher: Merion No. 342-40108 Price: 30¢

Voicing: two-part[1] Grade: easy Time: 0:45

Accompaniment: a cappella

Type of Text: secular

Range and Tessitura: not applicable

Avant-garde:

inflected rhythmic speech (graphic notation); whispering

Traditional:

Rhythm: eighth and quarter notes

[1]Choir divided into high and low voices

THREE-IN-ONE-IN-THREE

Composer: Richard Felciano Author: biblical

Publisher: E. C. Schirmer No. 2910 Price: 45¢

Voicing: SAB/SAB Grade: med. Time: 8:30

Accompaniment: electronic tape; organ, solo instruments - optional

Type of Text: sacred; trinitarian

Range and Tessitura:

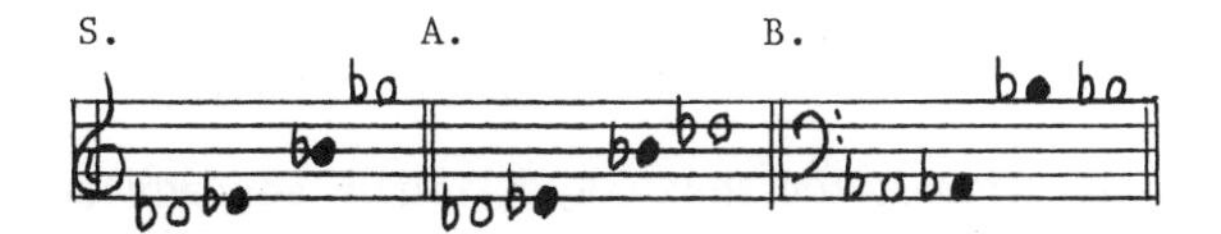

Avant-garde:

ad libitum use of musical fragments (cells), entrances; rhythmic speech; placement of choirs

Traditional:

Melody: tonal; along chord patterns; ostinato figures

Harmony: tonal; nonfunctional because of ad libitum elements

Rhythm: unmetered; traditional symbols used; combinations of eighths and sixteenths; syncopation

TIME IS NOW, THE[1]

Composer: Karl Korte  Author: Eve Merriam

Publisher: Elkan-Vogel  No. 362-03205  Price: $1.50

Voicing: SATB  Grade: diff.  Time:

Accompaniment: electric guitar; three radios - optional[2]

Type of Text: secular; novelty

Range and Tessitura:

Avant-garde:

inflected rhythmic speech; rhythmic speech and singing combined; glissandos; whispering; quarter-tones

Traditional:

Melody: nontonal; chromatic; isolated pitches at times; entrances difficult to hear; quarter-tones

Harmony: nonfunctional; fourths; major/minor seconds between adjacent voices; augmented, diminished octaves in many chords; altered chords of all types

Rhythm: changing meters (4/4, 3/4, 2/4, 5/4); triplet quarters, eighths; syncopation

---

[1]Four compositions; could be performed separately

[2]Piano score of voice parts for rehearsal

TIME TO EVERY PURPOSE, A

Composer: Gilbert Trythall Author: biblical

Publisher: Marks No. 4586 Price: 85¢

Voicing: SATB[1] Grade: diff. Time: 9:39

Accompaniment: electronic tape (supplies occasional pitch cue)[2]

Type of Text: sacred; Ecclesiastes; order in creation

Range and Tessitura:

Avant-garde:

rhythmic speech

Traditional:

Melody: tonal; conjunct; some chromaticism

Harmony: functional; major/minor seconds between adjacent voices; sevenths

Rhythm: changing meters (4/4, 5/4); syncopation; triplet eighths; combinations of eighths and sixteenths

[1]Audience participation desirable

[2]No reduction of voice parts

TO TROUBLED FRIENDS[1]

Composer: Daniel Pinkham Author: James Wright

Publisher: Ione No. 2942 Price:

Voicing: SATB div. Grade: diff. Time:

Accompaniment: string orchestra; electronic tape[2]

Type of Text: secular; variety of ideas

Range and Tessitura:

Avant-garde:

tone clusters; glissandos; inflected rhythmic speech[3]

Traditional:

Melody: nontonal; disjunct; chromatic; augmented, diminished intervals of all types

Harmony: nonfunctional; parallel fourths; major/minor seconds between adjacent voices; unison, two-part passages; chords built with seconds and sevenths prominent

Rhythm: changing meters (4/4, 2/4; 4/4, 6/8; 3/4, 4/4, 2/4, 5/8; 4/4, 5/4, 10/8, 9/8, 2/4); triplet eighths, quarters; three-against-two; combinations of eighths and sixteenths; much unison rhythmic movement

[1]Four movements; probably can be performed separately

[2]Tape used in only two movements

[3]Used in one movement; other three totally traditional in notation

TONGUE OF WOOD, A

Composer: Jack Boyd   Author: Stephen Crane

Publisher: G. Schirmer   No. 11511   Price: 40¢

Voicing: SATB, S. solo   Grade: med.   Time:

Accompaniment: a cappella

Type of Text: secular; acceptance by another

Range and Tessitura:

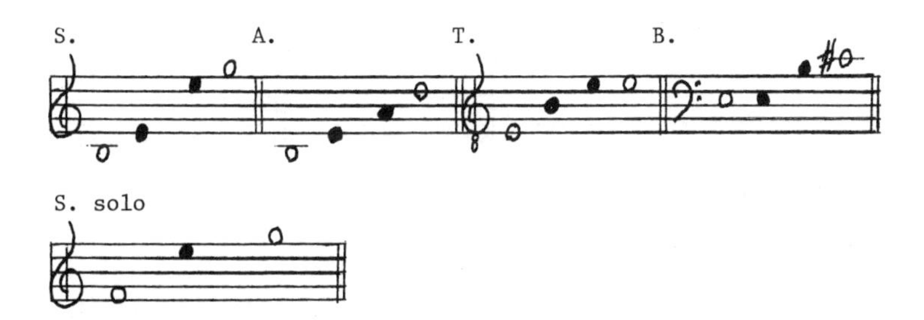


Avant-garde:

rhythmic speech; finger snaps

Traditional:

Melody: tonal; disjunct

Harmony: functional through repetition of patterns; augmented, diminished chords; major seconds between adjacent voices; open fourths, fifths

Rhythm: changing meters (3/4, 4/4); syncopation; combinations of eighths and sixteenths

[1]Solo very short (eight and half beats)

TOWER OF BABEL

Composer: Nevett Bartow Author:

Publisher: Shawnee No. A-1002 Price: $1.25

Voicing: SATB div.; STBB solo Grade: diff. Time: 12:00

Accompaniment: piano; timpani; snare drum; gong; glockenspiel; xylophone; wood block; tom-tom; suspended cymbal; siren (slide-whistle); cowbell; ratchet; triangle; tambourine[2]

Type of Text: sacred; biblical story of tower of Babel[3]

Range and Tessitura:

Avant-garde:

rhythmic speech; ad libitum shouting, screaming; create confusion

Traditional: variety of styles present

Melody: tonal, nontonal; chromatic; conjunct, disjunct

Harmony: functional, nonfunctional; major/minor seconds between adjacent voices; open fifths, octaves; unisons

Rhythm: changing meters (3/4, 2/4, 4/4, 3/8, 5/8, 4/8, 6/8); syncopation; combinations of eighths and sixteenths; much unison rhythmic movement

---

[1]Second movement TBB

[2]Percussion parts - $4.00 per set

[3]Foreign languages sung by soloists; phonetic spelling supplied

TRAVELOG[1]

Composer: Brent Pierce | Author:

Publisher: Walton | No. 2924 | Price: 60¢

Voicing: three-part choir[2] | Grade: med-easy | Time:

Accompaniment: piano;[3] flute; woodblock; tom-tom; Jew's harp; drum; tambourine

Type of Text: novelty; syllables; vowel, consonant sounds; various countries

Range and Tessitura:

Avant-garde:

rhythmic speech; inflected rhythmic speech; murmur; flutter tongue glissandos; lip smacking; sighing; laughing; tone cluster; glottal stops; tongue clicks; vibrato; choreography; graphic notation of pitch; rhythmic speech and singing combined

Traditional:

Melody: tonal; modal; ostinato melodic patterns; chromatics; minor second prominent

Harmony: functional; ostinato patterns; major/minor seconds between adjacent voices

Rhythm: one movement changing meters (alternating 3/4, 4/4); combinations eighths and sixteenths; syncopation

[1]Six movement suite

[2]Equal or unequal voices; variety of voicings for different movements

[3]Pianist needs facility; must read accidentals

TROIS POEMES A CRIER ET A DANSER: CHANT I

Composer: Keith Humble  Author: Pierre Albert-Birot

Publisher: Universal  No. 29049  Price: 50¢

Voicing: SATB, div.  Grade: med-easy  Time:

Accompaniment: claves (metal and wood), maracas, music boxes, clickers, bottles

Type of Text: novelty; syllables, vowels, consonants

Range and Tessitura:[1]

Avant-garde:

ad libitum selection of musical events, entrances; tone clusters (some written-out); approximate pitch; flutter tongue, rhythmic speech; laughing; whispering; shouting; humming; lip pops; foot stamps; knee slaps; finger snaps; hissing

Traditional:

Rhythm: triplet eighths, quarters; syncopation; unmetered sections

[1]Only pitches specified

TROIS POEMES A CRIER ET A DANSER: CHANT II

Composer: Keith Humble    Author: Pierre Albert-Birot

Publisher: Universal    No. 29050    Price: 50¢

Voicing: SATB    Grade: med-easy    Time:

Accompaniment: claves, maracas, music boxes, clickers, bottles

Type of Text: novelty; vowels, consonants

Range and Tessitura: relative to individual singer

Avant-garde:

tone clusters; rolled "R"; glissandos; vibrato; modification of sound with hands; alternating vowel sounds; rhythmic speech; foot-tapping (ad libitum rhythm)

Traditional:

Rhythm: triplet eighths against four sixteenths

TROIS POEMES A CRIER ET A DANSER: CHANT III

Composer: Keith Humble    Author: Pierre Albert-Birot

Publisher: Universal    No. 29051    Price: 50¢

Voicing: SATB    Grade: med-easy    Time:

Accompaniment: claves (wood, metal); maracas; music boxes; clickers; bottles

Type of Text: vowels, consonants

Range and Tessitura: not applicable

Avant-garde:

rhythmic speech; tone clusters; flutter tongue; vibrato; hand claps; modification of sound with hands; graphic notation of pitch

Traditional:

Rhythm: combinations of eighths and sixteenths; triplet eighths

TURBA

Composer: Miklós Maros    Author: biblical

Publisher: Hansen    No. WH - 109    Price: 75¢

Voicing: SATB div.; Mezzo soloist[1]    Grade: diff.    Time: 5-6:00

Accompaniment: a cappella

Type of Text: sacred; syllables; vowels, consonants; Beatitude: mourning

Range and Tessitura:[2]

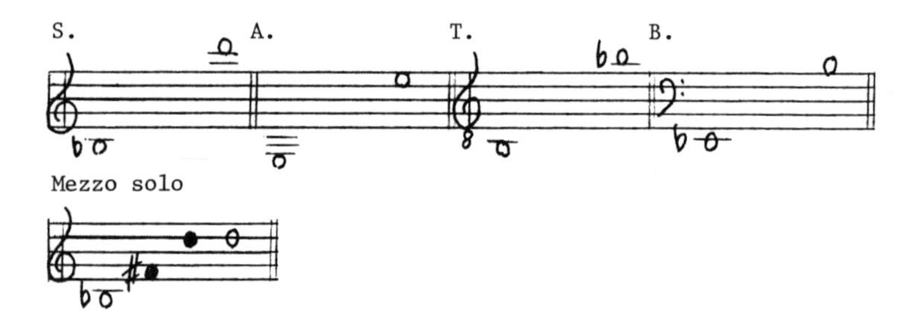


Avant-garde:

graphic notation of pitch, rhythm; improvise melody, rhythm

Traditional:

Melody: nontonal, microtones; isolated pitches; probably need pitch pipes; little melody in accepted sense

Harmony: nonfunctional; isolated chords; almost written-out tone clusters

Rhythm: not applicable

[1]Score calls for a solo voice from each sub-section for isolated pitches; also to perform a "chorale"

[2]Ranges include isolated pitches to be sung by solo voices out of each section; no tessitura given because of improvisational nature of much of the singing

TWO MOVES AND THE SLOW SCAT

Composer: Dennis Kam | Author:
Publisher: Belwin/Mills | No. Oct 2282 | Price: 35¢
Voicing: SATB | Grade: easy | Time:
Accompaniment: a cappella
Type of Text: syllables, vowels, consonants
Range and Tessitura: relative to individual singer

Avant-garde:

time segments; graphic notations of pitch, rhythm, dynamics; ad libitum pitch, rhythm

Traditional:

Rhythm: traditional symbols used, but without traditional meaning because of the ad libitum element

UNKNOWN, THE[1]

Composer: Michael Hennagin | Author: Stephen Crane[2]
Publisher: Walton | No. M-120 | Price: $2.50
Voicing: SATB, 4T. 3B. solo[3] | Grade: med. | Time:
Accompaniment: piano;[4] flute;[4] gong; bass drum; two tom-toms; suspended cymbal; vibraphone; electronic tape;[5] two slide projectors; three trumpets (play unison); timpani
Type of Text: secular; anti-war

Range and Tessitura:

Avant-garde:

rhythmic speech; inflected rhythmic speech; free chanting in rhythm; whispering; shouting; ad libitum pitch, use of text; glissandos

Traditional:

Melody: tonal; modal; shifting tonalities; conjunct

Harmony: tonal; many unison, two-part passages; major seconds formed from unisons; open and parallel fourths, fifths

Rhythm: changing meters (4/4, 5/4, 2/4, 3/4, 6/4, 5/8); unmetered section (traditional notation used); syncopation; triplet quarters, eighths; combinations of eighths and sixteenths

---

[1]A composition of five movements

[2]Also Walt Whitman, Carl Sandburg

[3]Soloists chant, sing in unison; range within choral range

[4]Facility needed by pianist and flutist

[5]Tape - $10.00

UNKNOWN, THE

Composer: Michael Hennagin Author: Walt Whitman

Publisher: Walton No. 2802 Price: 60¢

Voicing: SSA Grade: med. Time:

Accompaniment: piano;[1] flute;[1] gong; bass drum; two tom-toms; suspended cymbal; vibraphone

Type of Text: secular; mourning the dead

Range and Tessitura:

Avant-garde:

rhythmic speech; inflected rhythmic speech; free chanting in rhythm; whispering

Traditional:

Melody: modal; conjunct; chord patterns

Harmony: many unison, two-part passages; major second formed from unisons; fourths, fifths, sevenths

Rhythm: changing meters (4/4, 5/4, 2/4, 3/4, 6/4); syncopation; triplet eighths; combinations of eighths and sixteenths

[1]Facility needed by pianist and flutist

VALSE

Composer: Ernst Toch Author:

Publisher: Belwin/Mills No. 60564 Price: 75¢

Voicing: SATB div. Grade: med. Time: 3:45

Accompaniment: optional: side drum, chinese wood blocks, xylophone, wooden drum; claves

Type of Text: secular; novelty

Range and Tessitura: not applicable

Avant-garde:

rhythmic speech; inflected rhythmic speech

Traditional:

Rhythm: syncopation; tempo moderately fast with eighths, quarters, dotted halfs

VISION, THE

Composer: Dale Jergenson Author: Lawrence Ferlinghetti

Publisher: G. Schirmer No. 11880 Price: 50¢

Voicing: unspecified; seven soloists[1] Grade: easy Time:

Accompaniment: a cappella

Type of Text: secular; serious; vision of evil

Range and Tessitura: not applicable

Avant-garde:

speaking; shouting; hissing; special positions for choir; improvisation; graphic notation of pitch (inflection) rhythm; whispering

Traditional: not applicable

[1]Soloists improvise to text; they also speak, shout, whisper

VOICES NO. 1

Composer: Leonardo Balada Author:

Publisher: G. Schirmer No. 12023 Price: 75¢

Voicing: SATB div. a 3 Grade: diff. Time: 7:00

Accompaniment: a cappella

Type of Text: vowel and consonant sounds

Range and Tessitura:

Avant-garde:

tone clusters[1] (formed by written-out lines); whistling; whispering; approximate pitch notation; graphic pitch notation; oscillating tone; glissandos

Traditional:

Melody: nontonal; chromatic; major/minor seconds and thirds; octave leaps for basses; at times ostinato-like figures

Harmony: nonfunctional; extreme dissonance; seconds, thirds between adjacent voices; long pedal points in all voices; cluster sounds from unisons and back to unisons prominent

Rhythm: syncopation; triplet eighths

[1]At times notated as approximate pitches

VOICES OF THE DARK

Composer: Lyle Davidson Text: biblical

Publisher: E. C. Schirmer No. 2943 Price: 25¢

Voicing: SATB[1] Grade: easy Time: 6:00

Accompaniment: electronic tape;[2] optional - any five from the following: bass clarinet, trombone, tuba, harp, cello, double bass, piano, organ (do not have to be five different types)

Type of Text: sacred; Jeremiah 4:23-26; desolation

Range and Tessitura:

Avant-garde:

ad libitum rhythm, tempo, dynamics

Traditional:

Melody: descending Phrygian scale

---

[1]Mixture of voices unimportant; should have at least sixteen singers

[2]Tape available

WHAT DID YOU LEARN AT THE ZOO?[1]

Composer: Philip Hagemann Author: John Ciardi
Publisher: Presser No. 312-41128 Price: 60¢
Voicing: two-part treble Grade: med. Time:
Accompaniment: piano[2]
Type of Text: secular; humorous
Range and Tessitura:

Avant-garde:

inflected rhythmic speech; rhythmic speech; glissandos

Traditional:

Melody: tonal; chromatic; major/minor seconds between adjacent voices; cross voices

Harmony: functional; voice parts often major/minor second against accompaniment; parallel thirds, fourths between adjacent voices

Rhythm: changing meters (2/4, 6/8; 4/4, 2/4, 5/4, 3/4; 4/4, 2/4); triplet eighths; combinations of eighths and sixteenths

---

[1]Consists of three compositions; can be performed separately; No. 3 consists of all rhythmic speech unison

[2]Piano part includes voice pitches

WHERE SHALL I FIND THE CHRIST CHILD?

Composer: Max Exner
Author:

Publisher: Abingdon
No. APM-852 Price: 65¢

Voicing: SATB; speaking choir[1]
Grade: easy Time:

Accompaniment: temple blocks (low, medium); cymbal; snare drum; tom-tom; bass drum

Type of Text: sacred; Christmas - Nativity

Range and Tessitura:

Avant-garde:

rhythmic speech

Traditional: Hymn - "O Little Town of Bethlehem" in traditional notation

Rhythm: syncopation; triplet eighths

[1]Solo speakers; a variety of timbres is desired

WINDHOVER, THE

Composer: John Paynter
Author: Gerard Manley Hopkins
Publisher: Oxford
No. X 205
Price:
Voicing: SATB div.
Grade: diff.
Time: 5:30
Accompaniment: a cappella[1]
Type of Text: secular; mood; pictorial
Range and Tessitura:

Avant-garde:

improvisation on supplied pitches; improvisation against metered, traditional music; ad libitum use of text, length of improvisation

Traditional:

Melody: tonal; disjunct; chromatic; augmented, diminished intervals; crossed voices

Harmony: nonfunctional; seconds, sevenths, augmented, diminished intervals between adjacent voices

Rhythm: changing meters (2/4, 5/8, 3/8, 3/4, 4/4, 6/8); triplet eighths, quarters; polyrhythms; syncopation; combinations of eighths and sixteenths

[1]No reduction of voice parts

WORDS OF ST. PETER

Composer: Richard Felciano Author: biblical

Publisher: World Library No. CA 2093-8 Price:

Voicing: SAATB Grade: med-diff. Time:

Accompaniment: organ,[1] electronic tape

Type of Text: sacred; 1 Peter 2:1-9; call to follow Christ

Range and Tessitura:

Avant-garde:

perform with electronic tape (everything performed by choir traditionally notated)

Traditional:

Melody: nontonal; chromatic; disjunct (organ usually has pitches)

Harmony: nonfunctional; augmented, diminished chords; chords with added notes

Rhythm: changing meters (4/4, 5/4, 3/4, 2/4); syncopation, triplet eighths; combinations of eighths and sixteenths; each voice part independent, organ often parallels rhythmic motion of voice parts

[1]Rhythmic facility needed

ZODIAC

Composer: Bert Konowitz, Orlando DiGirolamo Author:

Publisher: Alfred No. 6111 Price: 50¢
Voicing: two-part[1] Grade: med-easy Time:

Accompaniment: piano; two-four tambourines

Type of Text: secular; description of zodiac characteristics

Range and Tessitura:

Avant-garde:

graphic notation of pitch; rhythmic speech; speaking; improvisation on supplied pitches; clapping; body movements

Traditional:

Melody: tonal; tonal shifts; repetition of melodic patterns

Harmony: functional; unisons; parallel thirds

Rhythm: syncopation

[1]Twelve small groups formed from the two main groups; each sub-section takes turn performing a unison improvisational section

ZOO: FIVE NONSENSE SONGS

Composer: Eskil Hemberg Author: Shel Silverstein

Publisher: Hansen No. 11841 Price: 35¢

Voicing: SATB div.;[1] T. solo Grade: diff. Time:

Accompaniment: a cappella[2]

Type of Text: secular; novelty

Range and Tessitura:

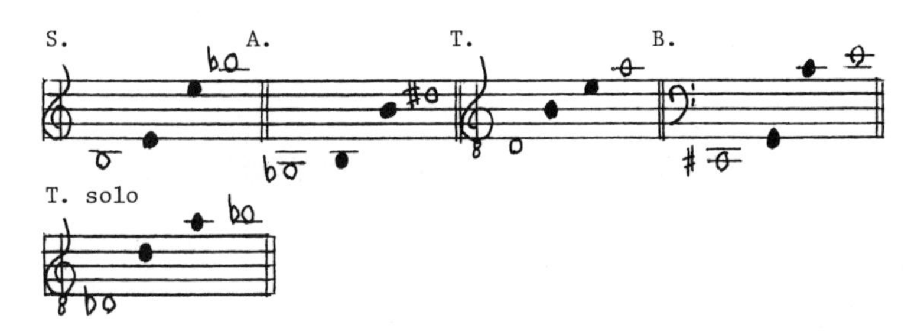


Avant-garde:

glissandos; rhythmic speech; inflected rhythmic speech; ad libitum rhythm, use of text; screaming; improvisation

Traditional:

Melody: nontonal; chromatic; most movement by major/minor seconds

Harmony: nonfunctional; augmented, diminished chords; parallel minor seconds between adjacent voices; chords built up to "cluster" sound

Rhythm: changing meters (6/8, 3/4); triplet eighths, sixteenths; syncopation; ties over measures, beats to fractions of following beats; unmetered section

---

[1]No. 1 - SSATB div.; all others SATB div.

[2]No reduction of voice parts

## PUBLISHERS' NAMES AND ADDRESSES*

| Code | Address |
|---|---|
| Abingdon | Abingdon Press<br>201 Eighth Avenue South<br>Nashville, TN 37202 |
| Agape | Agape<br>380 S. Main Place<br>Carol Stream, IL 60187 |
| Alfred | Alfred Publishing Co., Inc.<br>75 Channel Drive<br>Port Washington, NY 11050 |
| AMP | AMP [Associated Music Publishers]<br>866 Third Avenue<br>New York, NY 10022 |
| AMSI | Art Masters Studios, Inc.<br>Minneapolis, MN 55408 |
| Apogee | Apogee Press, Inc. (World Library) |
| Associated | see AMP |
| Augsburg | Augsburg Publishing House<br>426 S. Fifth Street<br>Minneapolis, MN 55415 |
| Beacon Hill | Beacon Hill Music (Belwin/Mills) |
| Belwin/Mills | Belwin/Mills Publishing Corp.<br>Melville, NY 11746 |

*Agents' names appear in parentheses after the publishers' names, where appropriate.

| | |
|---|---|
| Boonin | Joseph Boonin, Inc.<br>P. O. Box 2124<br>S. Hackensack, NJ 07606 |
| Boosey-Hawkes | Boosey and Hawkes<br>Oceanside, NY 11572 |
| Bourne | Bourne Company<br>1212 Avenue of the Americas<br>New York, NY 10036 |
| Broude | A. Broude, Inc.<br>1619 Broadway<br>New York, NY 10019 |
| Continuo | Continuo Music Press, Inc. (Broude) |
| Crescendo | Crescendo Publications, Inc.<br>P. O. Box 28218<br>Dallas, TX 75228 |
| Elkan-Vogel | Elkan-Vogel, Inc. (Presser) |
| C. Fischer | Carl Fischer<br>56-62 Cooper Square<br>New York, NY 10003 |
| Flammer | Harold Flammer, Inc.<br>Delaware Water Gap, PA 18327 |
| Foster | Mark Foster Music Co.<br>Box 4012<br>Champaign, IL 61820 |
| Galaxy | Galaxy Music Corp.<br>2121 Broadway<br>New York, NY 10023 |
| Galliard | Galliard, Ltd. (Galaxy) |
| General | General Words and Music Co. (Kjos) |
| Gentry | Gentry Publications (Presser) |
| Gray | H. W. Gray Co. Inc. (Belwin/Mills) |
| Hansen | Wilhelm Hansen Edition (Walton) |

| | |
|---|---|
| Heritage | The Heritage Music Press<br>Lorenz Industries<br>501 E. Third St.<br>Dayton, Ohio 45410 |
| Hinshaw | Hinshaw Music, Inc.<br>P. O. Box 478<br>Chapel Hill, NC 27514 |
| Hope | Hope Publishing Co.<br>Carol Stream, IL 60187 |
| Ione | Ione Press, Inc. (E. C. Schirmer) |
| Kjos | Neil A. Kjos<br>525 Busse Hwy.<br>Park Ridge, IL 60068 |
| Mark Foster | *see* Foster |
| Marks | Edward B. Marks Music Corp. (Belwin/Mills) |
| MCA | MCA (Belwin/Mills) |
| Merion | Merion Music Co. (Presser) |
| New Music | The New Music Company, Inc.<br>1036 Shady Way<br>P. O. Box 126<br>Wichita, KA 67201 |
| Oxford | Oxford University Press<br>200 Madison Avenue<br>New York, NY 10019 |
| Pallma | Pallma Music Company (Kjos) |
| Pepper | J. W. Pepper<br>Valley Forge, PA 19481 |
| Peters | C. F. Peters<br>373 Park Avenue South<br>New York, NY 10011 |
| Piedmont | Piedmont Music Company, Inc. (Belwin/Mills) |

| | |
|---|---|
| Plymouth | Plymouth Music Co., Inc.<br>17 West 60th Street<br>New York, NY 10023 |
| Presser | Theodore Presser Co.<br>Presser Place<br>Bryn Mawr, PA 19010 |
| E. C. Schirmer | E. C. Schirmer<br>112 South Street<br>Boston, MA 02111 |
| G. Schirmer | G. Schirmer, Inc.<br>866 Third Avenue<br>New York, NY 10022 |
| Shawnee | Shawnee Press<br>Delaware Water Gap, PA 18327 |
| Somerset | Somerset Press<br>Carol Stream, IL 60187 |
| Southern | Southern Music Company<br>1100 Broadway<br>New York, NY 10019 |
| Staff | Staff Music Publishing Co., Inc.<br>(Plymouth) |
| Un. of Miami | University of Miami<br>dist. by Sam Fox Pub. Co., Inc.<br>1540 Broadway<br>New York, NY 10036 |
| Universal | Universal Edition (Boonin) |
| Walton | Walton Music Corp.<br>17 West 60th Street<br>New York, NY 10023 |
| Warner | Warner Brothers Publications<br>1230 Avenue of the Americas<br>New York, NY 10020 |
| Weinberger | Joseph Weinberger (Boosey-Hawkes) |
| Westwood | Westwood Press, Inc. (World Library) |

| | |
|---|---|
| World Library | World Library Publications, Inc.<br>2145 Central Parkway<br>Cincinnati, OH 45214 |

## INDEX OF WORKS FOR SATB

This index includes works, both a cappella and accompanied, for SATB and combinations of SATB divisi. A cappella -- *

## INDEX OF WORKS FOR SAB

This index includes works, both a cappella and accompanied, for SAB, or those which can be adequately performed by an SAB choir; A cappella -- *

## INDEX OF WORKS FOR SSA (SSAA)

This index includes works, both a cappella and accompanied, for treble voices (changed and unchanged). A cappella -- *

## INDEX OF WORKS FOR TTB (TTBB)

This index includes works, both a cappella and accompanied, for the male choir, or which can be performed by it. A cappella -- *

## INDEX OF WORKS FOR TWO-PART CHOIRS

This index includes works, both a cappella and accompanied, for SA, TB, or SB choirs, or works which can be performed by such choirs. A cappella -- *

## INDEX OF WORKS FOR UNISON CHOIR

This index includes works, both a cappella and accompanied, for unison choir, or which could be performed by a unison choir. A cappella -- *

## INDEX OF WORKS FOR SPEAKING CHORUS

This index includes works which are written for speech choirs. The number of parts is shown in parentheses.

The two works below can be performed by speaking choir in as much as the works employ only "body sounds" (clapping, finger snaps, etc.)

# INDEX OF WORKS WITH ELECTRONIC TAPE ACCOMPANIMENT

This index includes the works which use electronic tape accompaniment either as the sole accompaniment, with other instruments, or as an option. Optional -- * (N. B. Though not marked some works can be performed without the electronic tape accompaniment.)

## COMPOSER INDEX

## BIBLIOGRAPHY


### BOOKS

Cope, David. New Directions in Music. Dubuque, Iowa: Wm. C. Brown Company, Publishers, 1971.

Decker, Harold A. and Julius Herford (eds.). Choral Conducting: A Symposium. Englewood Cliffs, N.J.: Prentice-Hall, Inc., 1973.

Garretson, Robert L. Conducting Choral Music. 3d ed. Boston: Allyn and Bacon, Inc., 1970.

Karkoschka, Erhard. Notation in New Music: A Critical Guide to Interpretation and Realization, trans. Ruth Loening. New York: Praeger Publishers, 1972.

Lamb, Gordon H. Choral Techniques. Dubuque, Iowa: Wm. C. Brown Company, Publishers, 1974.

Nardone, Thomas R., James H. Nye, and Mark Resnick (eds.). Choral Music in Print. Philadelphia, PA.: Musicdata, Inc., 1974.

Pooler, Frank, and Brent, Pierce. New Choral Notation: A Handbook. New York: Walton Music Corporation, 1971.

Read, Gardner. Music Notation. 2d. ed. Boston: Allyn and Bacon, Inc., 1969.

Risatti, Howard. New Music Vocabulary: A Guide to Notational Signs for Contemporary Music. Urbana, IL.: University of Illinois Press, 1975.

### PERIODICALS

Archibeque, Charlene Paulin. "Developing a Taste for Contemporary Music," Journal of Research in Music Education, XIV (Summer, 1966), 142-47.

Behrman, David. "What Indeterminate Notation Determines," Perspectives of New Music, III (Spring/Summer, 1965), 58-73.

Ehle, Robert D. "Romanticism in the Avant-garde: Leon Kirchner's Piano Sonata," The American Music Teacher, XIX (April/May, 1971), 30-31.

Hirt, Charles C. "The Sounds of Things to Come," The Choral Journal, IX (November/December 1968), 8-11.

Jones, Perry O. "Reactions to Brock McElheran's 'Patterns in Sound'," The Choral Journal, XI (September, 1970), 12-13.

Lamb, Gordon H. "Indeterminate Music for Chorus," The Choral Journal, X (May, 1970), 12-15.

McElheran, Brock. "Beginner's Guide to the Avant-garde," The Choral Journal, XIII (April, 1973), 19-24.

Pooler, Frank. "Where Are We Going?" The Choral Journal, XVI (September, 1975), 5.

Stone, Kurt. "Problems and Methods of Notation," Perspectives of New Music, I (Spring/Summer, 1963), 9-31.

Struckmeyer, Eva Mae. "An Approach to 'Avant-Garde' Music for the Beginner," The Choral Journal, XIV (October, 1973), 7-8.

Talley, Mike. "Knut Nystedt's Compositional Style as Analyzed in 'Praise to God'," The Choral Journal, XV (September, 1974), 12-13.

Thoburn, Crawford R. "Electronic Media and the Amateur Chorus," The Choral Journal, XII (September, 1971), 11-14.

Thompson, Edgar J. "Comments on Avant-Garde Choral Music: An Interview with Frank Pooler," The Choral Journal, XII (December, 1971), 9-14.

Wilkey, Jay W. "Krzysztof Penderecki's Dies Irae," The

Choral Journal, X (March, 1970), 14-16.

Wuorinen, Charles. "Notes on the Performance of Contemporary Music," Perspectives of New Music, III (Fall/Winter, 1964), 1-21.

Zetty, Claude. "Choral Music in the Curriculum: The Choral Music of Paul Hindemith," American Choral Review, XI (January, 1970), 28-35.

UNPUBLISHED

Hicks, Val J. "Innovative Choral Music Notation: The Semantics, Syntactics and Pragmatics of Symbology." Unpublished doctoral dissertation, University of Utah, 1971.

Potter, Gary Morton. "The Role of Chance in Contemporary Music." Unpublished doctoral dissertation, Indiana University, 1971.

Temko, Peter Michael. "The Perception of Pitch Predominance in Selected Musical Examples of Avant-Garde Composers; 1945-1961." Unpublished doctoral dissertation, The Florida State University, 1971.

Wollman, William A. "The Effect of a Contemporary Compositional Process Derived from Aleatory Techniques on the Musicality of College Level Non-Music Majors." Unpublished doctoral dissertation, New York University, 1972.